THE BANTU
CIVILIZATION OF
SOUTHERN AFRICA

THE BANTU CIVILIZATION OF SOUTHERN AFRICA

By E. Jefferson Murphy

Illustrated by Louise E. Jefferson

THOMAS Y. CROWELL COMPANY
New York

By the Author:

THE BANTU CIVILIZATION OF SOUTHERN AFRICA
HISTORY OF AFRICAN CIVILIZATION
UNDERSTANDING AFRICA

*The drawing on page 253 is based on an illustration
in* African Art-The Years Since 1920, *by Marshall Ward Mount,
published by the Indiana University Press in 1973.*

DESIGNED BY MERI SHARDIN

Manufactured in the United States of America

Library of Congress Cataloging in Publication Data

Murphy, E Jefferson.
The Bantu civilization of southern Africa.

Bibliography: p.
1. Bantus.   I.   Title.
GN656.M87   916.8'06'963   73-17194
ISBN 0-690-00399-4

1   2   3   4   5   6   7   8   9   10

For Terry, Kathy, and Patrick

Maps

Contents

Bakongo cup

Preface

Americans, like most Western people, have only recently begun to learn that Africa has a long and proud history. For a long time our knowledge of that history was confined to the colonial period and the exploration of Africa by adventurous Europeans. Egyptologists studied the awesome mysteries of the great Nile civilization, but considered it separate from the rest of Africa.

In the past few years more attention has been given to the glorious past of the West Africans. More and more people are becoming familiar with the great empires of Ghana, Mali, and Songhai, recognizing that in them black Africans created their own proud civilization. Yet the history of much of the rest of Africa is still only vaguely known, and it is often assumed that most of Africa outside the Nile Valley and West Africa achieved very little in its past.

This book is devoted to telling the story of the impressive development of a distinctive civilization in another part of Africa, that part that lies below the equator. Almost all the continent south of the equator is inhabited by peoples who speak languages of the widely dispersed Bantu language group. Today these peoples live in more than a dozen countries, between Uganda and South Africa on the east and Cameroun and Namibia on the west. The differences among them are obvious. They speak hundreds of languages, live in nations that are geographically and politically separate, and range from wealthy to poor.

Scholars of Africa's past have learned that all these peoples, no matter how diverse they may seem, are united by deep ties of language, culture, and history. They share a common origin, dating back more than two thousand years.

Because they have followed differing paths of development, these peoples of central and southern Africa have no single name, other than that of their language. Their languages belong to the group known as Bantu, so that it is customary to refer to them as the Bantu-speaking peoples. In the modern Republic of South Africa, where the European settlers rule and oppress the indigenous African population, it has become fashionable to use the term "Bantu" to refer to the country's Africans. In this case the term is used to avoid calling them "Africans," which to the whites implies more dignity than they want to accord. Further, the Dutch-descended whites of South Africa call themselves "Afrikaners," which means "Africans," and they fiercely resist any confusion between themselves and the blacks whom they suppress so arrogantly.

In this book, which is inspired by admiration for the historical achievement of the Bantu-speaking peoples, the term "Bantu" is rarely employed to refer to the people, but rather to their languages and their civilization. Where the term is used to refer to the people, it is because there is no other word readily available. The author does not accept the condescending attitudes of South Africans, or confuse a linguistic title with a race or a people.

The Bantu civilization includes many notable accomplishments. Its people conquered, for the most part peacefully, more than a third of the entire African continent. They developed highly organized kingdoms and empires, within which millions of people were wisely ruled. Their artists created brilliant sculpture in clay, stone, metals, and wood. Their farmers were wise in their knowledge of how to conserve precious water and soil fertility, and were able to grow scores of vegetables, grains, and root crops. They knew how to mine iron, copper, gold, tin, and other metals, and to work these metals into fine tools and ornaments. They learned how to weave cotton into fine cloth, and to use the wool and skins of animals when cotton was not available. Their religious beliefs were complex. Their poetry, mythology, riddles, folklore, and literature, though not written down until recently, were beautiful and graceful.

The peoples who produced and were shaped by

the Bantu civilization have proved themselves worthy to stand among the great peoples of the world. Although their lands were often arid or infertile, they made the best of the conditions they found, and established the Bantu civilization with skill and creativity. This book is the story of its origins and development, and of the great kingdoms and empires its peoples built in Africa south of the equator.

"Kasai velvet," Baluba

THE BANTU
CIVILIZATION OF
SOUTHERN AFRICA

1

The Bantu-Speaking
Peoples

Late in the year 1482, ten years before Columbus led his three small ships to the New World, a Portuguese captain named Diogo Cão sailed three battered, sea-worn little ships into the estuary of a great river on the western coast of central Africa, and there anchored to seek fresh water and food. The river, which the local peoples called Zaire, soon came to be known to Europe as the Congo. The populous black peoples whom Diogo Cão met there, and with whom he soon established cordial relations, identified themselves as subjects of the *Mani Kongo,* or "king of the kingdom of Kongo."

Diogo Cão did not know it, but he was the first known European to visit the lands of the far-flung peoples whom we call today the Bantu-speaking peoples. After Cão's visits (he made two later voyages to Kongo as well) hundreds of European ships, from England, France, Holland, Denmark, Sweden, Prussia, and other countries joined those of Portugal in calling at points along the Atlantic and Indian Ocean coasts of Africa south of the equator, establishing contact with new groups of Africans, each of which seemed different in many respects from the others. For nearly four hundred years Europeans dealt with the many peoples of Africa south of the equator without recognizing that they were all closely related, one group to another, despite apparent differences in language, dress, way of living, political organization, and race.

Europe was so impressed with the wealth, pageantry, and obvious lordliness of the king of Kongo and his court that they often spoke of his country as the most civilized in Africa. Nor was Kongo the only kingdom that demanded the respect of Europe; as early as 1500, and up until the 1860's, Europeans continued to find still other highly civilized states in the interior of central and southern Africa—their kings powerful and commanding, their armies numerous, and their exports of gold, ivory, and copper impressive.

Not all the peoples of southern and central Africa earned such favorable European reactions, however. Many, both along the coasts and in the interior, spent much of their time herding cattle, producing little wealth and giving no evidence of the kind of complex political organization which was so distinctive in Kongo, Mwene Mutapa, Changamire, Buganda, and some other states. Europeans eventually came to look down on these pastoral, less materially developed peoples, especially after the first permanent European settlements were founded in South Africa, and the European colonists began to realize that their guns and ammunition gave them power over the Africans whose lands they coveted.

Yet today we know that almost all the African peoples south of the equator, whatever early Europeans may have thought of them, are members of one great language group, sharing a common history and a common civilization. The modern countries of Angola, Botswana, Burundi, Cameroun, Congo (Brazzaville), Gabon, Kenya, Lesotho, Malawi, Mozambique, Namibia (South-West Africa), Republic of South Africa, Rhodesia, Rwanda, Swaziland, Tanzania, Uganda, Zaire (formerly called Congo, with the capital at Kinshasa), and Zambia are all largely populated by Bantu-speaking peoples, and there are other Bantu speakers living in a few neighboring countries. All together nearly one-third of the peoples of Africa, or roughly 100 million, speak one or another of the Bantu languages.

These numerous and widely dispersed peoples cover roughly one-third of the African continent; their territory totals more than 4 million square miles, a land mass more than twice as large as Europe, and a little larger than the United States including Alaska.

3

In many ways the differences among this huge group of peoples seem more impressive than any similarities. They differ widely in racial composition, for example. Some are short and slight of build, with yellowish or light brown skins and facial features which set them apart from the more Negroid peoples of West Africa. Others exhibit evidence of long mixture with Caucasoid peoples, so that they now have brown skins and wavy hair. Still others are closely similar to the Negroid peoples of West Africa, with dark brown skins, tightly curled hair, fleshy lips, and broad, flat noses. Some are unusually tall, with men averaging over six feet, and have tightly curled hair and dark skins but thin lips and sharp noses. Little wonder that Europeans could remain ignorant, for four centuries, of the common origins and underlying unity of civilization of such heterogeneous peoples.

By the mid-nineteenth century missionaries and scholarly travelers had learned a number of African languages and recorded them in dictionaries and grammars. European philologists (students of language) realized, upon comparing these languages, that most of those in central and southern Africa were remarkably similar in structure and word forms. One of the earliest of these scholars, Wilhelm Bleek of Germany, coined the term *Bantu* when he found that almost every language spoken in south and central Africa used the same word, *Abantu*, to refer to "men" or "the people." In these same languages *Amuntu*, the singular form of the same word, was universally used to mean "a man."

Bleek, and other scholars who followed him, found that the Bantu languages showed their common ancestry in many other ways as well. Almost all contained a core of common words (although the words had begun to change form in some, as in European languages the Latin *uno* has changed to *one, ein, un,* etc.). All formed the difference between singular and plural by changing the prefix, and prefix changes were also used to indicate the agreement of adjectives, pronouns, and verbs with the nouns to which they referred. In the decades that have followed the work of Bleek and other philologists, most of the Bantu languages have been studied, and each newly studied one reflects the same basic characteristics as the others. Today between three hundred and four hundred Bantu languages are recognized; it is impossible to be precise as to the number, since scholars often do not agree on whether certain languages are sufficiently different from others to be called separate languages rather than dialects.

These three or four hundred languages differ from each other in varying degrees. Some are as dissimilar as French and Rumanian, while others are closer than Spanish and Portuguese. Although we say that the numerous Bantu languages are "mutually unintelligible," meaning that a person speaking one cannot converse with a person speaking another, this tends to overstate their dissimilarity. It has been found that a person from Zululand, for example, can go to Uganda, more than two thousand miles away, and learn the language sufficiently to carry on a limited conversation within a few weeks. The deep common roots and the basic similarities in structure and vocabulary are as real as the differences, clearly.

5

Until the essential unity of the Bantu languages was recognized, Europeans were far more impressed by the elements of diversity among the Bantu-speaking peoples. Even today Europeans who are skeptical of African capabilities or who have negative images of Africans prefer to stress their differences. Thus in white South Africa it is a widespread belief among the ruling group that the subordinate African majority is composed of a number of separate tribes, each speaking its own language and each far more concerned with its tribal identity than with any sense of unity with other Africans.

As we will see, in later chapters, there is indeed much variety among the multitudinous Bantu-speaking peoples. The more intensively one studies them, however, the more one is struck with the essential uniformity of their religions, world views, ideas about life, and attitudes about political and social organization—and the fact of their common origins. And despite their diversity, they are bound together by a history which is one of the most exciting and fascinating sagas in the history of all mankind.

The history of the Bantu-speaking peoples is unusual because it is one of constant migrations from several points of origin. In these numerous and complex migrations small groups of Bantu colonists spread themselves, together with their languages and their common civilization, over the vast area that they now occupy, in little more than a thousand years. For the most part they quickly absorbed, usually by intermarriage, the more primitive peoples who inhabited the area before they came. In a few cases the Bantu themselves adopted much of the culture of the indigenous peoples, and in other cases a fusion of cultures resulted. The settlement of this vast region in such a comparatively short space of time represented a population movement of epic proportions; in sheer scale it is comparable to the settlement of the Americas by the ancestors of the Indians, the explosions of the Arab peoples following the birth of the Muslim religion, and the worldwide colonization by Europeans after the Age of Discovery in the fifteenth and sixteenth centuries.

Reconstructing the historical process by which the Bantu speakers spread themselves so widely, establishing their civilization in each new area, is an intellectually demanding task. Yet it is a thrilling one, somewhat like unraveling an intricate puzzle. Had the Bantu-speaking peoples used writing, the task might have been far less difficult, and perhaps less exciting as well. But with a few isolated exceptions they used no writing until the past century or so, and they moved so extensively that they built few of the great stone edifices and monuments that have helped so much to unravel the history of Egypt, Sumeria, and other early civilizations.

In the absence of writing, and with few enduring monuments of stone, how have scholars been able to reconstruct Bantu history? As we shall see, they have used great ingenuity, ferreting out bits and pieces of information from archeology, linguistic analysis, anthropology, botany, zoology, chemistry, and other sciences, combining this information with the oral histories passed on from one genera-

7

tion to the next in almost all Bantu societies. The result is far from a neat historical picture, with all important details filled in. Yet it is equally far from being vague guesswork. The major routes of migrations, the reasons for undertaking them, and the methods by which they were carried out, as well as the accomplishments of the Bantu speakers in each of their new homelands have been sketched out well enough so that most scholars are in agreement. Research continues, and each new piece of information is quickly fitted into the overall outline; sometimes new information requires a significant change in the broad outline of Bantu history, but more often it serves to fill in missing detail and to clarify unclear areas.

Before we begin the story of the ancient Bantu-speaking peoples, it will help if we look briefly at the modern Bantu peoples and the lands in which they live.

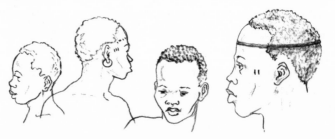

Moving south from eastern Nigeria, near the border between Nigeria and Cameroun, one very quickly reaches Bantu country. Many of the peoples in the eastern part of Nigeria speak languages which are related to the Bantu group, though they are not sufficiently similar to be classed as Bantu languages. In the northwestern part of Cameroun (and on the offshore island of Fernando Po) live many peoples speaking different Bantu languages, including the Duala, from whom comes the name of Douala, one of Cameroun's leading cities. Farther south live one of the first large groups, the Fang, who spread over a wide territory of Cameroun and adjacent Gabon. In Gabon and Congo (Brazzaville) live numerous other Bantu speakers, one of the more numerous being the Teke (more properly, the Bateke; many Bantu-speaking peoples use the prefix *ba* as the plural for their group, while an individual is indicated by the prefix *m, am,* or *um.* For simplicity we will generally not use the prefixes).

Immediately to the south of the lands of the Teke and related groups are the Kongo, whom Diogo Cão visited and from whom both the river and the modern country have taken their name. Inland, due east from the Kongo, live the Chokwe, Lunda, and Luba, each of which has achieved special prominence in African history. These peoples are among the more numerous and influential in modern Zaire (as the Congo [Kinshasa] renamed itself in 1971), as well as in Angola.

In both Angola and Namibia (the official name for South-West Africa) there are numerous Bantu groups, with the Mbunda of Angola and the Ovambo and Herero of Namibia being best known.

In the modern Republic of South Africa, together with neighboring Botswana, Lesotho, and Swaziland, most of the Bantu-speaking peoples belong to societies that speak either Sotho languages (as do the people of Lesotho and Botswana) or Nguni languages (including those of the Zulu, Xhosa, and Swazi).

9

Much of Rhodesia and parts of Mozambique are dominated by various widely dispersed clans of Shona peoples, but other groups are also important. In Rhodesia live the Matabele (or Ndebele), a group of Nguni speakers who invaded and conquered part of Shona territory in the nineteenth century. Both in Rhodesia and in southern Mozambique are the numerous Tonga-speaking peoples; they are divided, like the Nguni to their south, into several language groups.

Farther north, in Malawi, Zambia, Tanzania, and northern Mozambique, live large numbers of Bantu-speaking peoples. Most are divided into moderate-sized language groups, of whom a few of the more notable are the Lozi and Bemba of Zambia; the Yao, found in both Malawi and Tanzania; and the Chewa, found in Malawi and Zambia. Still farther north, both Burundi and Rwanda are populated by Bantu-speaking peoples.

Tanzania contains dozens of Bantu-speaking groups, none being nationally prominent; the Sukuma and Nyamwezi are among the most populous. Neighboring Kenya is inhabited by both Bantu-speaking peoples and peoples of a quite different origin, the Nilotics. Among the Bantu speakers the most prominent are the Kikuyu and the Wakamba.

Like Kenya, Uganda contains large numbers of both Bantu- and Nilotic-speaking peoples, with the Bantu-speaking Baganda (from whom the modern country took its name) being the most numerous and prominent.

Small groups of Bantu-speaking peoples migrated even farther north, beyond the equator, into modern Somalia. Still others are found in the

Tunis

Algiers

Rabat

MOROCCO

TUNISIA

Mediterranean Sea

Tripoli

Cairo

SPANISH
SAHARA

ALGERIA

LIBYA

EGYPT

N

MAURITANIA

MALI

NIGER

CHAD

Khartoum

Nile River

AFARS & ISSAS

Nouakchott

Dakar

SENEGAL

Bamako

Fort Lamy

SUDAN

ETHIOPIA

SOMALI
REPUBLIC

GAMBIA

GUINEA-
BISSAU

UPPER
VOLTA

Niamey

Ouagadougou

ETHIOPIA

Addis Ababa

Freetown

GUINEA

NIGERIA

SIERRA LEONE

IVORY
COAST

GHANA

DAHOMEY

Lagos

CENTRAL
AFRICAN REPUBLIC

Mogadiscio

Monrovia

Abidjan

Accra

TOGO

CAMEROUN

Bangui

LIBERIA

EQUATORIAL
GUINEA

Yaoundé

UGANDA

KENYA

Libreville

GABON

ZAIRE

Nairobi

RWANDA

BURUNDI

CONGO
(Brazzaville)

Brazzaville

Kinshasa

TANZANIA

ZANZIBAR

Dar es Salaam

*Indian
Ocean*

Luanda

MALAWI

Atlantic Ocean

ANGOLA

ZAMBIA

Lusaka

Salisbury

MOZAMBIQUE

MADAGASCAR

Tananarive

NAMIBIA

RHODESIA

BOTSWANA

Gaberones

SWAZILAND

AFRICA

1974

Countries shaded are inhabited wholly
or mainly by Bantu-speaking peoples.

Jefferson.

SOUTH AFRICA

LESOTHO

Capetown

Central African Republic, in the center of the African continent east of Cameroun.

Finally, located along the Indian Ocean coast between southern Mozambique and Somalia, live dozens of relatively small Bantu-speaking groups who have had close contact with Arab traders and settlers for more than a thousand years. Out of this long contact grew a distinctive culture and language, the Swahili, which helps to lend uniformity to the peoples over nearly two thousand miles of coastline. Their culture is clearly Bantu, and the Swahili language is Bantu. But Arab customs and words have been blended with Bantu in the Swahili area to produce a unique civilization.

The perceptive reader may have noticed that so far the term "tribe" has not been used to describe any of the Bantu-speaking peoples. The use of the word "tribe" can be so misleading and inaccurate that it is best to avoid it entirely, instead using such terms as "group," "society," "ethnic group," "population," or "language group." Very few of the peoples in any part of Africa live in what we think of as tribal groups. This fact is so important to our understanding of the history and achievements of the Bantu-speaking peoples that we must digress for a moment to clarify it.

The way in which Bantu-speaking Africans govern themselves has varied from region to region. But the great majority have lived in states headed by kings, so that we must recognize the kingdom as being the most typical kind of Bantu political organization.

Bantu social organization has typically been in small families, which are in turn part of lineages;

12

everyone in the lineage traces descent back, through many generations, to a common ancestor. When that descent is traced through the females of the family (from daughter to mother to grandmother, etc.), it is called "matrilineal," and the common ancestor of the clan is a woman. If descent is traced through the male line, as it is in most Bantu societies, it is called "patrilineal," and the common ancestor of the lineage is a man.

In Bantu societies these lineages may have tens, or even hundreds, of thousands of members, so that it is impossible for each person to trace his ancestry through every generation to the common ancestor. The members of the lineage simply assume that they have a common ancestor because the traditions of their lineage say so. Each lineage has a story, or myth, of how it came into being; the ancestor has a name, is believed to have been a person of unusual abilities, and is said to have performed many wonderful feats and to have possessed great wisdom.

When a powerful lineage moved into a new area, perhaps conquering the people who were already settled there, its prestige may have been so great that the conquered people eventually accepted the tradition of the ruling lineage's ancestor. Thus many of the lineages include people who are not really descended from the mythical ancestor, but who nevertheless believe that they are.

The social organization of lineages and the political organization of kingdoms are often, in Bantu society, two very different things. Peoples living in a kingdom may be of several different lineages, and the king is usually selected from one of the

13

lineages which is more powerful and prestigious than the others. It has occasionally happened that peoples of one large lineage are split between two different kingdoms.

When we use the term "tribe" we usually think of a people who speak a common language, share a common culture, recognize descent from the same ancestor, and acknowledge the authority of a common leader. This clearly is not the case in many Bantu societies. A number of lineages speak the same language and share a common culture but feel no close kinship to each other, inhabit separate territories, and may acknowledge completely different leaders. They may well recognize a vague connection because of the common language and customs, but often will feel that this is of no importance in their daily lives. The obligations of a person to his or her lineage or king usually are much more important than any obligation to other peoples who happen to speak the same language but are of different lineages or kingdoms.

Another reason it is misleading to use "tribe" is the fact that we associate the word with primitive society and behavior. As we will see in later chapters, the Bantu peoples were far from primitive in social organization, culture, or behavior. They were a civilized people, capable of creating elaborate kingdoms and empires; impressive tools, farms, and cities; great works of art and architecture; powerful poetry and oral literature; and religions with a Supreme Being and deep moral values.

Yet, as we have already noted, the Bantu peoples differed much from each other. In their migrations they came into close contact with many other peoples, and often absorbed customs and techniques from them. As they moved, constantly settling new lands farther and farther from their point of origin, they found many different geographical environments. Each of these environments called for new ways of tilling the soil and tending herds of cattle, sheep, or goats. And each new environment offered different challenges and opportunities. Some, such as present-day Rhodesia, Zambia, and Zaire, were rich in minerals, so that the Bantu peoples who settled there became proficient miners and workers of copper, tin, iron, and gold. Others were rich in stone that could be used for temples and public buildings, and in those areas the Bantu peoples erected impressive structures. Still others offered good grazing lands that were poorly suited to growing crops, and in these areas the Bantu came to rely heavily on their herds for a livelihood.

The result, after centuries of pioneering migrations, was a fascinating patchwork of cultures and ways of living. Yet at a deeper level, in social and political organization, religion, and philosophy, the underlying base of Bantu civilization could still be recognized. It is this complex blend of difference and uniformity which lends such excitement to the saga of the Bantu peoples.

15

2

Bantu Origins
and Migrations

Long after it was recognized that the Bantu-speaking peoples were of common origin, despite their variety and the vast territory they inhabit, their place of origin was unknown. Scholars began to suggest theories, usually based more on speculation than on scientific evidence, but there was little agreement among the numerous theories that began to appear as early as 1900.

One theory, based on the fact that most Bantu-speaking peoples in South Africa had legends which told of migrations from the north, held that they originated somewhere near the Great Lakes of East Africa, in the vicinity of Uganda. This theory suggested that the Bantu ancestors had, in very ancient times, been influenced by the Egyp-

16

tian civilization of the Nile River but had become increasingly primitive as they moved ever farther south from the source of civilization.

Another theory, influenced by the racial diversity of the Bantu-speaking peoples along the Indian Ocean coast and in parts of southern Africa, speculated that the Bantu peoples were the descendants of intermarriages between unknown Africans and immigrants from Egypt, Arabia, or the Far East.

It was not until the early 1950's that a theory of origin based on scientific evidence appeared. It grew out of the comparative studies of African languages by Joseph Greenberg, an American linguist and anthropologist. Greenberg assembled information on the vocabularies and grammars of most African languages. In comparing them, he found that the Bantu languages showed certain similarities to a cluster of languages spoken by peoples living between the high plateau of central Nigeria and the area of the Camerouns where the nearest of the true Bantu languages could be found.

Greenberg established clearly that the Bantu languages, numerous though they were, were related to other languages spoken throughout West Africa and could be classed as a division of the great African language family he named Congo-Kordofanian. Having established the relationship between Bantu and West African languages, a relationship which was closest in the area where Nigeria and Cameroun adjoin, Greenberg concluded that the ancestors of the Bantu had migrated southward from that area.

At about the same time a British linguist, Malcolm Guthrie, was engaged in painstaking research on the Bantu languages themselves. Using a large number of common word roots, he made statistical comparisons of the appearance of each word root in widely dispersed Bantu languages. From his analysis an interesting patte   emerged. The languages which had the largest number of basic word roots were Bemba and Luba, in the Katanga region of Zaire and adjacent Zambia; the farther away from this area a language was spoken, the fewer roots it had in common with the other Bantu languages analyzed.

While Guthrie's findings did not invalidate the relationship Greenberg had found between Bantu and West African languages, Guthrie concluded that the origin of Bantu languages (the "cradleland," as he termed it) was in the Katanga region of central Africa. Using statistical methods, he found evidence that other Bantu speakers had apparently migrated away from this cradleland, first to the east and west, then later to the north and south.

For a few years after the publication of these studies by Greenberg and Guthrie there was a lively controversy in scholarly circles. Some scholars, more persuaded by Greenberg's research, argued that the Bantu ancestors came from Nigeria and had fanned out southward to cover all of Africa south of the equator. Others, impressed by Guthrie's findings, insisted that the earliest Bantu speakers came from central Africa and migrated north and south.

In the past few years most scholars have devoted their energies to reconciling these two theories. It

18

is now generally accepted that the ancestors of the Bantu-speaking peoples did come from the Nigeria-Cameroun area, as suggested by Greenberg, but that they established a new home in the Katanga region and from there migrated outward in the pattern suggested by Guthrie.

The Nigeria-Cameroun homeland of the Bantu ancestors is a country of grasses and woodlands, with a moderate amount of rain each year. The people now living there grow corn, millet, beans, some rice, and various root crops such as cassava and yams. The Katanga region has a very similar geography and produces many of the same crops. Because of this close similarity in the two environments, it is logical that an agricultural people migrating from the Nigeria-Cameroun region would adapt easily and quickly to a new homeland in Katanga.

The story of the Bantu origins begins between 1000 and 500 B.C., when the population of West Africa was expanding into all arable areas and was beginning to overpopulate its territory. Nigeria was already, at that early date, an emerging center of cultural progress. Nigerian archeologists have uncovered rich evidence of a prosperous agricultural people with an impressive artistic tradition, centered on the Nigerian plateau only a few hundred miles north and west of the Bantu ancestral area.

By 500 B.C. there was considerable pressure to find new lands to support the expanding population of central and eastern Nigeria. The Atlantic Ocean blocked expansion to the southwest, and the great plains to the north and east were already occupied by agricultural peoples. The only possible

19

route of expansion lay to the south. In that direction stretch the vast tropical rain forests of the Congo Basin, a country of heavy rainfall, dense forests of towering trees, and numerous rivers, streams, and swamps. The rain forests were very sparsely populated at the time, because they were inhospitable to farming.

The need to find new lands eventually forced ambitious, adventurous pioneers to move into the Congo rain forests. It is likely that the first pioneers were fishermen, who knew how to build sturdy, large canoes from the giant trees of the forests. They are believed to have known agriculture as well, their women growing garden crops while the men fished. As early as 500 B.C. family groups of these fishermen-farmers were exploring the numerous streams and rivers of Cameroun, most of which flow southward into the great Congo River system. Setting up small villages in clearings along the waterways, they moved slowly but inexorably southward into the heart of the Congo region. Eventually they moved up other rivers and streams which flow west and north from their origins in Katanga and East Africa.

By about 100 B.C. parties of these pioneers are believed to have reached the Katanga area, where they found drier grasslands and forests similar to those of their ancestral homeland. Here the cultivation of grains and numerous vegetables was profitable, and fishing became a less important side activity. By about A.D. 100 the ancestral Bantu had established a rapidly growing new population center, based on farming, in the Katanga environment. From this region they continued to expand both eastward and westward, reaching the Atlantic Ocean and the Indian Ocean by about A.D. 400.

These early pioneers, moving restlessly generation after generation to found new settlements, must have been hardy and brave. And they were far from primitive in their knowledge of arts and crafts. Their relatives in central Nigeria had learned how to mine iron ore and smelt it to produce raw iron as early as 500 B.C., and from the raw iron they forged durable blades for hoes, axes, knives, and spears. If the pioneer ancestors of the Bantu peoples did not take this knowledge of ironworking with them on their migrations, they soon added it to their already formidable technology. With iron axes they were able to fell trees and clear new lands easily, and with iron weapons they could defend themselves from wild animals or the few hostile peoples they met in their migrations.

Archeologists have found evidence of ironworking in central Nigeria as early as about 500 B.C., and in central Africa, not far from the new Bantu cradleland, about A.D. 100. The moist earth and

21

dense vegetation of the Congo Basin have thwarted archeological research, however, and most of the relics the Bantu ancestors left in their journeys through that region have decomposed.

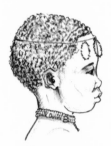

Khoisan child

Most of the new lands the Bantu ancestors settled were sparsely populated by peoples of the Khoisan language family, who have survived into historical times in southern Africa as the groups known to Europeans as Bushmen and Hottentots. (These are names coined by Europeans, and are never used by Khoisan peoples to refer to themselves.) The ancient Khoisan peoples lived over much of Africa from Nigeria and Ethiopia to the southern tip of the continent, but they were hunters whose way of life was much simpler than that of the Bantu. As the Bantu moved into the territories of the Khoisan peoples, they absorbed most of them by intermarriage, so that gradually these peoples disappeared except in the southernmost areas of Africa. Their yellowish skin color and physical features have survived in some Bantu populations, however, as has their unique use of clicks in speaking. Today certain large Bantu groups, such as the Xhosa and Zulu of South Africa, use Khoisan clicks in their languages; Miriam Makeba, the prominent African singer, has made these exotic click sounds familiar to all Americans who have heard her.

Zulu man

Since the Khoisan peoples were not farmers, there was no basis for conflict over territory between them and the immigrating Bantu. Even today small bands of "Bushman" hunters trade the game they have killed to Bantu farmers for grains and pottery, or work as laborers on Bantu farms.

Xhosa woman

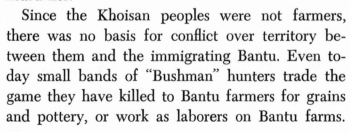

22

Over a long period the Khoisan peoples were absorbed into the stronger, more numerous Bantu populations, but it is not likely that the two groups were frequently at war with each other.

There has been too little archeological research yet done to establish with any accuracy the dates when the first ancestral Bantu speakers established settlements in the Katanga area. Most linguists believe that it would have taken roughly two thousand years for the Bantu languages to have reached their present state of diversity from each other, assuming they all stem from one ancestor language. This would suggest that the first group settled in Katanga between 100 B.C. and A.D. 100. This is, of course, a very rough estimate, and the correct date could be as much as two or three centuries earlier or later.

One archeological find, however, tends to confirm the estimate. In the Machili Forest Station of Zambia, several hundred miles southeast of the Katanga area, evidence of ironworking and pottery in the style of later Bantu peoples has been found, and dated at approximately A.D. 100. Similar finds still farther south, in Rhodesia (especially at the site of the famous stone ruins at Zimbabwe), date at about A.D. 300–400. And even farther south, in the Transvaal province of South Africa, further evidence of ironworking and pottery in the Bantu tradition has been dated at about A.D. 800–900.

Guthrie's linguistic analysis is thus supported, in rough outline, by archeology, especially in his conclusion that the people of the Katanga cradleland moved gradually south over a period of centuries.

By about A.D. 500 ancient Bantu-speaking peo-

Spearheads, Zimbabwe

23

BANTU ORIGINS AND MIGRATIONS: 500 B.C.—A.D. 1500

ORIGINAL
BANTU

500 B.C.

Atlantic Ocean

FOREST
BANTU
A.D. 500-1000

INTERLACUSTRINE
BANTU
A.D. 500-1000

NORTHEASTERN
BANTU
A.D. 500-1000

BANTU
CRADLELAND
A.D.-0

Indian Ocean

SOUTHWESTERN
BANTU
A.D. 1000-1500

SOUTHEASTERN
BANTU
A.D. 300-500

SOUTHERN BANTU
A.D. 1000-1500

Louise E. Jefferson

ples had settled a vast belt of central African lands stretching between the Atlantic and Indian oceans. They covered parts of the modern countries of Angola, Zaire, Zambia, Rhodesia, Malawi, and Mozambique. As they expanded they carried with them their practices of sowing millet and other grain crops, of fashioning good pottery, and of ironworking. In areas that had rich soil and ample rainfall they became densely populated and prosperous.

Soon offshoots of people, moving in small family groups of one or two men with their wives and children, were pressing north and south. They are known to have reached the rich farming country of southern Uganda before A.D. 1000, and had moved up the Indian Ocean coast into Somalia by about the same period. Arabic records from the period show that there were Bantu peoples living near Mogadiscio, the ancient city which is the capital of modern Somalia.

Other groups had entered what is today South Africa before A.D. 1000, and continued to move gradually south in that area until about A.D. 1500, when they reached their southernmost limit of expansion.

As the Bantu migrants fanned out in every direction from their cradleland, they followed those routes which were best for farming and avoided areas which were too dry or too swampy for their grain crops. In several large regions they bypassed inhospitable territories, moving into them only many centuries later when forced to do so by population pressure. One such area was central Tanganyika, a dry country with poor soil and unpre-

dictable rainfall. Another was southwestern Africa, much of which lies within the great Kalahari Desert. In that area Bantu-speaking peoples moved into the more favorable sectors of land in the highlands of central Namibia (South-West Africa), but left the arid sections along the coast and in the south to the Khoisan hunters.

Most of the ancient Bantu migrants passed through the Congo rain forests without establishing large settlements. It is believed that those who remained there were few in number, living in small settlements along the rivers and streams, eking out a living by fishing and a little farming. During the late part of the first millennium, however, and possibly after A.D. 1000, the continually expanding Bantu population of the Katanga cradleland region began to move into the rain forest in larger numbers, clearing lands away from the waterways and gradually building permanent farming communities.

They were able to undertake this new settlement of the rain forests because they had learned how to grow several tuber plants, notably yams and coco yams (taro), which had been imported into Africa from Indonesia during the first millennium. These plants, nutritious and high-yielding, grew well in areas of heavy rainfall, and are believed to have greater food value than the few native African tubers that the early Bantu knew how to grow. Using the Asian root crops as a basis for a new kind of agriculture, the Bantu-speaking peoples implanted themselves firmly in what had previously been inhospitable land. By the period A.D. 1300–1500 they were settled throughout the Congo Basin rain forests.

26

This new wave of immigrants, originating in the Katanga cradleland, apparently absorbed most of their distant relatives who had settled along the waterways many centuries before. Today the Bantu peoples of the rain forest speak languages which are relatively closely related to Luba, Lunda, Bemba, and others in the cradleland region, rather than to the "Bantoid" languages of the Nigeria-Cameroun area.

In their extensive migrations between about A.D. 100 and 1500 the Bantu-speaking peoples adapted themselves, where necessary, to the varied conditions they found in each new environment. By 1500 some, such as those in the Congo rain forest, lived by farming root crops. Others, such as the Luba, Lunda, Bemba, and many others in the savannas and dry woodlands, depended upon the cultivation of millet, eleusine (an Ethiopian grain somewhat similar to millet), sorghum, and vegetables. Still others, in the rich, well-watered country around Lake Victoria Nyanza, had learned to cultivate bananas and plantains for their main food supply.

In the many dry areas of central and southern Africa where grains do not produce good yields, many of the Bantu settlers switched to animal husbandry as a primary source of food, herding cattle, sheep, and goats. A few, forced by popula-

tion pressure into areas where cattle could not thrive, turned to hunting and gathering wild foods. Still others, who settled around lakes and waterways rich in fish, depended mainly on fishing and farming.

This quality of adaptability resulted in a mosaic of peoples whose life-styles were very different from each other. It was not until European students of language realized the close relationship among the languages of these otherwise dissimilar people that it could be recognized that they were of one basic stock. As more information has been accumulated, however, similarities other than language have become apparent: religion, philosophy, social organization, political organization, and many arts and crafts.

Where the Bantu peoples found hospitable new lands on which to settle, they sank deep roots which produced a proud civilization. Although all the Bantu-speaking peoples share a common origin and a similar potential for civilization, it was those groups who found rich soil and mineral resources who developed the impressive states and empires that are among the proudest Bantu achievements.

*Armorial shield
of the Kingdom of Kongo*

3
Kongo: The Dream
That Failed

The great kingdom that Diogo Cão visited was one of the most illustrious ever created by the Bantu-speaking peoples. And its centuries of close contact with Portugal, launched by Cão's mission, provide one of the most poignant examples of destructive European influence in African history.

The kingdom of Kongo was centered in the northern part of what is today the Portuguese colony of Angola. At its zenith it stretched more than 200 miles from north to south, between the modern Congo (Brazzaville) and the modern Angolan capital of Luanda, and roughly the same distance east to west, between the Atlantic Ocean and modern Kinshasa, the capital of Zaire. Within this region of 40,000 to 50,000 square miles the *Mani*

Kongo ruled supreme, while numerous lesser kings and chiefs around his borders paid him tribute and respected his considerable military and economic power.

Archeological research in the Kongo region is still too scanty to reveal the history of the peoples who lived there before the founding of the kingdom of Kongo. Yet there must have been a long period of development before this event, which has been dated at somewhere between A.D. 1325 and 1375. The ancestors of the Bakongo people were almost certainly living in or very near the area by A.D. 1000, speaking the Kongo language and supporting themselves, as their descendants did, by cultivating millet, cassava, beans, and vegetables, as well as by fishing in the Congo River and the other rivers and streams that flow through the area.

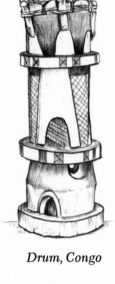

Drum, Congo

The early history of the kingdom itself is known only through the oral history or legend of the people, which weaves religious and mythical features into a generally factual account. According to the oral history, the kingdom was founded by a famous chieftain named Ntinu Wene, from whom most Kongolese claim descent. Historians believe that Ntinu Wene was a real man, and that he was indeed the first king who ruled over the powerful kingdom of Kongo. Oral history, however, endows him with semidivine status and magical powers, and claims for him many exploits which may be untrue or exaggerated. To understand how the Kongolese blend fact and fiction into the oral history it is necessary to understand something of their religion.

30

The Kongolese religion, once one understands it, is quite logical. It is based on a belief in a Supreme Being, whom the Kongolese call Nzambi Mpungu. He is believed to be a remote and omnipotent spirit who created all things, but who is so lordly and great that he created a variety of spirits to watch over the mundane affairs of men and earth. These spirits are of two kinds: the spirits of great ancestors and the spirits of nature. Nzambi Mpungu created nature spirits to govern the weather, crops, fire, rivers, disease, and other phenomena of nature. Man must be careful not to offend these spirits lest they punish him by bringing about famine, epidemics, floods, or other misfortunes.

Ancestor spirits are all the members of the family who have died, but only those who were especially good, wise, or powerful during life exercise important power as spirits. Their main function is to watch over the affairs of their descendants, rewarding those who do good and punishing those who do evil. The living must revere these powerful ancestor spirits, observe the family traditions and morals which they laid down, and sacrifice to them to show that they are remembered and respected. Because ancestors are powerful spiritual beings, legend tends to portray them as having had supernatural powers even when they were alive. Thus an important military victory by a revered chief of the ancient past may be attributed to his powers of magic as well as to his superior knowledge of military strategy and his bravery.

Kongolese oral history is based on chronological lists of kings and chiefs, in which the names and

31

exploits of each become the main content of the nation's history. Although modern scholars have been able to verify that these oral histories are based on real men and events, the powers and adventures of the more ancient rulers are undoubtedly exaggerated because of their having become, after death, important ancestor spirits within the Kongolese religion.

Ntinu Wene, as the founder of the kingdom, is a complex figure in Kongolese oral history. He is believed to have been a man, with all the vices and virtues which real men possess; he was capable of great charity, generosity, mercy, and wisdom, but he also, on occasion, was cunning, treacherous, and vengeful. The command over magical forces attributed to him makes him seem an awesome figure, whose good will men are anxious to attract, but whose ill will they try desperately to avoid.

Kongolese oral history tells nothing of the area and the people before Ntinu Wene. Yet there were certainly many extended families of Bakongo in the area before he arrived, each family headed by a chief whose power depended on the wealth and population of the lineage he headed. By A.D. 1200–1300 the more powerful of these chiefs were much like minor kings, each ruling his own territory of several thousand people. There must have been frequent tensions and conflicts between these petty kings and chiefs, as each struggled to expand his power and to secure his territory against encroachments from neighbors.

Throughout the area that the Kongo kingdom covers, as well as for hundreds of miles to the north, east, and south, small kingdoms seem to have

32

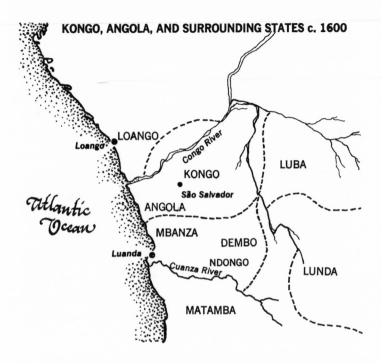

KONGO, ANGOLA, AND SURROUNDING STATES c. 1600

existed well before the fourteenth century. The legends of some peoples attribute the origins of their kingdoms to groups migrating into the country from the east, from the lands around Stanley Pool on the Congo River, where modern Kinshasa and Brazzaville are built. In a vast region of several hundred thousand square miles there may have been several dozen small kingdoms and chiefdoms in existence by about 1300, inhabited by Bantu-speaking peoples more or less closely related to the Bakongo.

From one of these small chiefdoms came Ntinu Wene, son of the chief of Bungu, with a troop of soldiers, onto the plains of Kongo south of the Congo River. He quickly subdued resistance, built a fortified capital at a town called Mbanza, and married a girl whose relatives were prominent spiri-

33

tual leaders of the area. His wife's kin accepted Ntinu Wene and hailed him as the *Mani Kongo,* or "King of the kingdom of Kongo." With this title, the support of the local aristocracy, a strong capital as base, and a seasoned army, Ntinu Wene began a campaign of conquest that within a few years allowed him to incorporate the chiefdoms of Mpemba, Nsundi, Mbamba, Mbata, Mpangu, and Soyo into his kingdom. These six lands became the six central provinces of the kingdom. Each was ruled by a governor, appointed by the *Mani Kongo,* except for Mbata, whose governor was automatically the hereditary head of the Mbata royal clan, since Mbata had voluntarily accepted Ntinu Wene's kingship.

The date of Ntinu Wene's death is unknown, although it was sometime between about 1375 and 1400. When he died, he left a strong and unified kingdom, ruled by a recognized government which was centered at the capital of Mbanza. Although other strong kingdoms flanked Kongo to the north, south, and east, none was capable of military threat to it, and several, such as Dembo, Ndongo, and Matamba to the south, sent annual tribute to Mbanza and usually supported Kongo in disputes with other kingdoms.

This was still the case a century later, when Portuguese ships began calling along the coast. Diogo Cão and those who followed him recognized that the *Mani Kongo* headed a powerful, well-organized, and wealthy state, the largest and most prestigious on the Atlantic coast of central Africa.

From the time of Diogo Cão on, numerous written records have survived to tell of the life of the

Kongo people, the affairs of their kingdom, and the ebb and flow of its national career. At the pinnacle of the state was the king, the *Mani Kongo*, the reigning monarch being Nzinga Kuwu during the early years of Portuguese contact. The king was believed by the people to have powers conferred on him by God that enabled him to safeguard the productivity of the kingdom's farms and the well-being of its subjects. Ordinary people were forbidden to observe him eating or drinking, on pain of death. The king was the head of the judicial system of the state, as well as of its political and religious structures. Only he could exact the death penalty for crimes, and other sentences could be appealed to him.

All male descendants of Ntinu Wene were legally entitled to the throne, and numerous factions and parties grew up around the more prominent and powerful heirs. Frequently, when an old king died, the leading heirs and their supporters came to blows with their rivals, although the winner—who was eventually crowned by a small committee consisting of the queen mother and a member of the royal cabinet—was accepted by all once his claims proved superior.

The king administered the country through a cabinet, made up of the governors of the six provinces, a retinue of personal aides, and a palace guard which served as the nucleus of the national army. Each of the governors headed an administration of provincial aides, district administrators, and village heads. Taxes were levied by the king, and collected by the provincial governors through their administrative subordinates.

The group around the king and his palace was large, and there was much pomp and pageantry designed to add to the king's majesty and dignity. He wore robes of office decorated with ostrich feathers, leopard skins, shells, and much gold and copper. His retinue included a host of personal aides, servants, and pages, in addition to governors, military commanders, wives, and the queen mother. Europeans, from the time of Diogo Cão on, were deeply impressed by the lordliness of the king and the size and complexity of his entourage.

The ordinary Kongolese was pleased by these marks of his king's power, wealth, and prestige, although his own life was humble in comparison. Most of the people were farmers and artisans, living in small villages of a few hundred or less, although many traveled to Mbanza, the capital, to marvel at the crowds and the pageantry of the court. Mbanza itself was a city, with a population of more than fifteen thousand, and its markets bustled with activity.

Most Kongolese lived by growing millet, sorghum, yams, bananas, beans, peas, watermelons, and many other fruits or vegetables, although a few fished and hunted to provide variety to the diet of their families. The soil was not rich, so the farmers used the typical African farming system of shifting cultivation. In this system the farmer selected a plot of a few acres at the beginning of the dry season, cut down all the trees and underbrush, and then burned them when they were dry. He then turned the earth with a hoe, mixing the ashes with the soil to add to its fertility. After harvesting one crop, he planted a different crop, until, after two or three years, the plot lost its natural fertility and the farmer moved to a nearby plot which had been similarly prepared. The exhausted plots were

left fallow for up to fifteen years, during which time weeds, small trees, and underbrush grew and helped to restore the plot's fertility.

Because of this system villages often moved from one spot to another, so that the farmers would be within easy walking distance of the plots being tilled. As the population of a village increased, small groups often moved farther away in search of less densely inhabited lands; this frequent movement, carried on over a period of centuries, was the basic pattern by which all the Bantu-speaking peoples migrated to populate southern Africa.

The necessity of shifting from one plot to another, and occasionally moving villages, discouraged the building of elaborate, permanent homes and the acquisition of numerous personal possessions. Most people lived in small houses of dried mud plastered on a wooden framework, with roofs made of woven grass, palm fronds, or reeds. They valued their pots, weapons, tools, clothing, and jewelry, and a few simple items of furniture such as cots, chests, and stools, all of which were easily moved. Many also treasured fine carvings of wood or stone by Kongolese artists, which symbolized revered ancestors.

After the Portuguese came, life changed somewhat, even for the ordinary farmer, because the Portuguese brought new crops from the New World: maize, tomatoes, potatoes, pineapples, tobacco, and manioc. These crops added to the produce of Kongolese farms, and some, such as maize, were so valuable that they became more important than the plants earlier cultivated. The Portuguese and other Europeans who came later also brought a variety of new goods: knives, scissors, needles, nails, guns, fine cloth, shoes, mirrors, and rum. Even though the Kongolese craftsmen knew how to produce most of these goods themselves, those brought by the Europeans were much less expensive, so after several centuries much of the craftsmanship of Kongo deteriorated.

Although the bulk of work in all of Kongo was carried out by the Kongolese peasants and artisans, the kingdom had long used slaves as workers. Slaves were people from other kingdoms who had been captured in wars, or occasionally Kongolese who had committed serious crimes or rebelled against the authority of the throne. Most slaves were owned by the king, the royal family, or the

Bawayo comb, Zaire

powerful nobility who governed the provinces and districts. These high-born people used slaves to farm their lands and to maintain their households. Slaves were also frequently used as soldiers, domestic servants, and personal assistants. In traditional Kongo society slaves had a legally recognized status and were protected by law from inhumane

39

Prester John

treatment or separation from their wives and children, unless they disobeyed their masters.

When the Portuguese first arrived in Kongo, they were exploring the Atlantic Ocean coasts of western Africa in search of a sea route to the Indies and the legendary lands of Prester John. Prester John was believed to be a powerful Christian king, whose kingdom was thought to be located somewhere in Africa (or in India), surrounded by hostile Muslim powers. The Portuguese believed that they might form an alliance with Prester John to crush the power of Islam, which had long dominated northern Africa and the Middle East and which stood between Europe and the rich trade of the Far East. As the Portuguese explored Africa in search of Prester John and a route to the Indies, they were also alert to opportunities for trade in Africa, and it was the wealth and majesty of the

Kongo court which led them to hope that lucrative trade might be carried on there.

Portuguese traders quickly recognized potential profits in the ivory, gold, silver, copper, and slaves which were so abundant in the Kongo capital. The slave trade had already begun farther north, because slaves were needed to work in Spain and Portugal and to serve as farm laborers on the rapidly expanding plantations of the Canary Islands, Madeira, São Thomé, and other Atlantic islands off the coast of Africa. Within a few decades after the first Portuguese ships began calling at Kongo, that kingdom was selling as many as four thousand slaves a year to eager Portuguese slave traders.

The first few decades of contact between Portugal and Kongo were dominated by the slave trade and the reign of one of the most remarkable kings in African history: Kongo's Affonso I. Affonso's forty-year reign witnessed such dramatic developments that it is still the favorite theme of Kongolese storytellers.

When Diogo Cão first visited Kongo, the reigning king was Nzinga Kuwu. He welcomed the visitors, and on Cão's second visit in 1485 willingly sent four of his noblemen back with him to Portugal, in exchange for four missionaries who had been brought to preach Christianity. Over the next few years several Portuguese expeditions came to Kongo, each time bringing new missionaries, traders, and artisans, and returning to Portugal with Kongolese ambassadors and students. In 1491 Nzinga Kuwu embraced Christianity and was baptized as King João I; most of his family and court were baptized along with him.

41

One of Nzinga's sons who accepted Christianity was Nzinga Mbemba, head of the province of Nsundi, who took the Christian name Affonso when he was baptized. His mother, the queen mother of the kingdom, took the name Eleanor.

A few years after accepting Christianity Nzinga Kuwu and one son renounced the new faith, reverting to the traditional Kongolese religion, but Eleanor and Affonso remained loyal Christians. When the old king died, in 1506, Affonso was forced to battle for the throne against his non-Christian brother, who had a larger army. According to Kongolese legend, Affonso easily vanquished the opposition because God sent angels to fight with his troops, and in late 1506 the devoutly Christian Affonso I became Kongo's new monarch.

Affonso was both a shrewd politician and a visionary leader. He persuaded the chief priest of the traditional faith to accept Christianity, at least in outward appearance, and put him in charge of all Catholic relics and holy objects. He proclaimed that his right to rule was blessed by the God of the Christians, and called on all Kongolese to accept the new faith. To help with conversions and instruction in Christianity he wrote to the king of Portugal, Manuel I, to ask for large numbers of priests, teachers, doctors, masons, and carpenters, who would set up schools, build churches, spread the gospel, and help care for the sick.

Many documents survive to tell of Affonso's effort to transform Kongo into a modern Christian kingdom; there are even twenty-two letters written by Affonso himself to Portugal's King Manuel and his successor, João. These accounts and letters make

42

it clear that Affonso was a deep believer in Christianity, and that he hoped to use Portuguese knowledge to educate his people, improve their health, and expand the wealth and prestige of his kingdom. He sent ambassadors to Rome as well as to Portugal, seeking papal recognition of his throne as Christian. And, wise in the ways of politics, he was also fully aware that many Portuguese traders and men of power were more interested in exploiting his country than in helping it become a great Christian force in Africa. Throughout a reign of forty years he remained steadfast in his faith and his vision of a greater Kongo, despite constant intrigue, internal dissension, and efforts by the Portuguese to subvert his authority and thwart his noble campaign of national development.

One of Affonso's first acts was to change the name of his capital from Mbanza to São Salvador. He built a large church of stone and mortar, a school for the children of the nobility, and residences for

Antonio, marquis of Nigritia, King Affonso I's ambassador to the Vatican (from a bust in S. Maria Maggiore, Rome)

the priests and teachers he had requested from Portugal. He continued to send young men to Europe for education—one of whom, his own son Dom Henrique, became a priest and a delegate to Rome and eventually was consecrated as the first Kongolese bishop.

The chief opposition to Affonso's grand design came from an alliance of his own vassals and Portuguese traders in São Thomé, the nearest and most powerful Portuguese base. The governor of São Thomé had been granted a Portuguese royal charter to control the trade with Kongo, and was growing wealthy on this trade and the burgeoning sugar production of his fertile island. His numerous trading agents in Kongo resented Affonso's efforts to maintain close relations with Lisbon and to secure Vatican recognition, and they found ready allies among the many district noblemen of Kongo who preferred to trade directly with the Portuguese without Affonso's supervision.

By 1526 the situation was so bad that Affonso wrote to Lisbon to complain that the São Thomé traders were conspiring with his vassals to kidnap Kongolese citizens into slavery, including even members of the royal family. He beseeched his brother king in Lisbon to help him rectify this sad state of affairs, indicating that he might ban the entire slave trade if matters did not improve.

Things were made worse by the ineffectiveness of the missionaries, teachers, and artisans sent by Portugal. They were few in number, and many became infected by the avarice for quick profits that motivated the Portuguese traders. Almost all the priests owned slaves and engaged in the buying

44

and selling of slaves. They set a poor example of Christian enlightenment, and were feeble instruments for carrying out Affonso's dream of converting his kingdom to a powerful Christian nation.

History shows that Affonso failed in his great design; not until the past few decades have the Kongo people begun to forge ahead in education and technological development. Yet his accomplishments were impressive. He made Europe aware of the fact that there were kings of vision and power in the heart of Africa. He enlarged his kingdom, maintained internal order and peace, and exercised strong influence over powerful kingdoms beyond his borders. In the face of the constant intrigues between Portuguese slave traders and avaricious Kongolese vassals, restive under Affonso's progressive regime, his long reign alone testifies to his skills as a leader. His dream of a great Christian Kongo was doomed by the forces arrayed against it, the forces that valued profits and exploitation more highly than nobler goals. But his faith, courage, vision, and political genius left their stamp on Kongo's history, serving as a shining example to countless later generations of the greatness that once was.

Affonso died about 1545, but the exact date and cause of his death are unknown. He was succeeded briefly by Pedro I, a relative who enjoyed the strong support of the Portuguese powers in São Thomé, but the Kongolese people rebelled and installed Affonso's grandson, Dom Diogo I, as the legitimate king. So great was their respect for Affonso's memory that after his death no man could be crowned unless he could prove that he was a direct descendant of Affonso, through one of his two sons or his one daughter.

Diogo I was an able king, ruling very much in the same style as his grandfather, but was constantly beset by the same problems of Portuguese intrigue and rebellious vassals. He reigned from 1545 until his death in 1561. One major event during his reign was the successful declaration of independence by the kingdom of Ndongo, a strong neighboring state which had previously acknowledged Kongo's overlordship.

Ndongo lay nearly three hundred miles to the south of Kongo, along the Atlantic Ocean coast and to some distance into the interior. It was founded formally in about 1500, and its first kings, called *Ngola*, sent occasional tribute to São Salvador and allowed much of its trade to flow through Kongo,

Woven grass house, Congo

although rather unwillingly. Late in the reign of Affonso I Portuguese traders came in increasing numbers directly to Ndongo, and the *Ngola* attempted to establish relations with both Lisbon and São Thomé. Officially Lisbon was bound by a treaty with Kongo which prohibited direct Portuguese relations with Ndongo, but São Thomé encouraged direct trade and contact. In 1556 Diogo raised a Kongolese army to march against Ndongo, hoping to force the *Ngola* to cease his efforts to bypass Kongo. When the two armies met, Ndongo was successful, dealing a severe defeat to Diogo's troops and forcing them to withdraw back to Kongo. From this time on Ndongo regarded itself as a completely sovereign kingdom, and Kongo was unable to prevent it from trading directly with Portugal and São Thomé.

Diogo's defeat proved to be a blow to the powerful reputation Kongo enjoyed in central Africa, and it also opened the path to the later Portuguese invasion of Ndongo and the conquest of the port of Luanda. In 1575, at a period when Kongo itself was at war with invaders from the interior, Portuguese troops landed at Luanda, seized the port, and began a campaign to conquer Ndongo which lasted for nearly a century. With the conquest of Luanda, however, Portugal gained a permanent foothold on the coast of central Africa which has lasted until today; Luanda is the bustling modern capital of the Portuguese colony of Angola (whose name comes from the ancient title *Ngola*).

Diogo died in 1561, and was succeeded by several kings whose reigns were troubled and brief. In 1567 Alvare I became king. Almost as soon as he began to consolidate his power and restore internal order, the kingdom was invaded by fierce contingents of Jaga warriors from deep in the interior. The exact origin of the Jaga is unknown, but they are believed to have been a group of warriors related to the Luba and Lunda of central Zaire and

47

Angola, who migrated from their homeland during a period of internal upheaval in order to seek their fortunes among the prosperous kingdoms to the west. The Jaga soldiers moved rapidly, recruiting both troops and wives among groups whom they conquered. They are known to have been skillful fighters who employed a variety of tricks and strategies to defeat larger forces. Between about 1560 and 1580 they ravaged nearly a thousand miles of land between Loango, north of Kongo, and the Cunene River, far to the south of Benguela in modern Angola.

When the Jaga fell upon Kongo, Alvare's troops were quickly defeated, and he was forced to seek refuge on an island in the Zaire (Congo) River. The Jaga roamed the Kongo countryside, razing crops and terrorizing the people. Repeatedly Alvare called upon Portugal for aid, but it was not until 1571 that an army was sent, under the command of the governor of São Thomé, to assist him. By this time the country was in a state of near-prostration. The Jaga had seized thousands of people, including many members of the nobility, for sale to Portuguese slave traders, and famine gripped the land.

The São Thomé army, six hundred men armed with arquebuses, marched with Alvare's troops against the Jaga and, after four years of battle, expelled them from Kongo. During this period the Portuguese virtually ruled the country, and Alvare had little power to do anything but work with them in the task of defeating the Jaga.

It was during this period of Portuguese occupation of Kongo that Portugal invaded Ndongo, confident that Alvare could make no protest. When the Portuguese forces withdrew from Kongo in 1576, Alvare began to restore his kingdom to order, while the Portuguese concentrated their attention on the war against Ndongo and the establishment of a permanent base there.

Alvare was able to use the peace brought to Kongo with great profit. He moved rapidly to re-establish his government, and prosperity quickly returned as the farmers planted their crops and internal order prevailed. There is some evidence that Alvare, in his appeals for aid against the Jaga, had promised to surrender Kongo's sovereignty to Portugal; upon the return of peace, however, he made it clear that he intended to restore Kongo to its earlier glory in every respect, and to guard against too much Portuguese influence in its affairs. In this effort he was successful; when he died, in 1584, the kingdom was as strong and united as it had ever been.

Alvare I's policies were continued by his son and successor, Alvare II, one of the last of Kongo's great kings. Both monarchs sought more priests, teachers, and technicians from Portugal, Spain, and other European countries, and both strove to gain Vatican recognition of Kongo as a Christian power. In this campaign Alvare II was successful. During his reign, between 1584 and 1614, the Pope received

49

permanent ambassadors to Rome from the *Mani Kongo*. Alvare II also decreed that Portuguese titles of nobility be used officially in Kongo, that Portuguese be the official court language, and that Portuguese dress and etiquette be approved for noble Kongolese.

Despite Alvare's success in gaining Vatican recognition and his encouragement of Portuguese styles at the court in São Salvador, he was unable —like his father—to secure enough help from Portugal to make the major economic progress he sought. Few missionaries and teachers were sent; of these, many died each year of tropical diseases, and others succumbed to the opportunities to acquire wealth and power through the slave trade. By the time Alvare II died in 1614, there was little more change outside the court than had been achieved by Affonso I, a century earlier, when the modernization program had been first conceived.

The sad fact is that the modernizing ambitions of Kongo's kings from Affonso I on were inconsistent with the desire of Portugal to reap profits from Kongo and other central African kingdoms through the slave trade. Portuguese kings and high church officials signed generous treaties with Kongo, and made numerous pronouncements about their sincere wish to aid in the development of Kongo as an enlightened, progressive Christian nation. But their words were belied and subverted by the avarice of wealthy men in Lisbon, Madrid, and São Thomé, and by the corruption and ineffectiveness of most of their emissaries to Kongo.

For more than a century Portugal regarded Kongo as too strong for outright invasion and conquest. But Portugal's wealthy slave traders and plantation owners resented the efforts by Kongo's kings to regulate the slave trade and the behavior of Portuguese traders in the kingdom, and they campaigned constantly to persuade Lisbon to restrain the Kongolese kings. The Portuguese invasion of Ndongo and the establishment of a base at Luanda were the first permanent successes of this anti-Kongolese policy. With a Portuguese foothold in central Africa next door to Kongo, Portuguese economic interests could operate without the interference of Kongo's kings.

The Portuguese invasion of Ndongo altered the balance of power in central Africa slowly but surely. Before about 1575 the affairs of Kongo had been decided by internal forces and by the ebb and flow of the relationship with Portugal and São Thomé. After 1575 relations with Ndongo and the Portuguese governor at Luanda became matters of vital importance as well. For a time Kongo tended to support the Portuguese wars against Ndongo (which lasted for nearly a century before Ndongo was finally conquered and the colony of Angola was securely under Portuguese control), because it had long regarded Ndongo as a vassal state. In 1581, for example, Alvare I sent an army to assist the Portuguese against Ndongo, but it was defeated.

During the 1580's Kongo began to realize that a strong Portuguese presence in Angola was dangerous, and under Alvare II it began to support the Ndongo cause. In 1589 Alvare entered into an alliance with Ndongo, and the allied states enlisted the support of Jaga chieftains and the inland state of Matamba. In that year their combined

51

armies met the Portuguese army and severely defeated it, driving it back to the sea, where it took refuge in the fort at Luanda. For some reason which no record clarifies, the African allies did not follow up their victory, but instead allowed the Portuguese to remain in Luanda unmolested. For many years afterward there were temporary alliances between Kongo and Ndongo which allowed both kingdoms to resist Portuguese conquest, although they were never powerful enough to dislodge the Portuguese from Luanda and other footholds in Angola.

After about 1600 the situation became even more complex, when the Dutch began to interest themselves in central African affairs and the slave trade. Throughout the sixteenth century Holland had been ruled by Spanish kings (who also, during the same period, ruled Portugal), but it gained its independence in wars between 1572 and 1609. Protestant, anti-Spanish forces had driven Spain out of northern Holland during the 1570's and had built an energetic commercial system which was sending Dutch ships all over the world seeking to break the trade monopoly of Spain and Portugal; one area of great interest to these Dutch merchantmen was the western coast of Africa.

By 1622 Kongo had developed so many contacts with Dutch traders that it was clearly allied with the Dutch against the Portuguese, despite protests from Lisbon, Madrid, and Rome. This alliance was bitterly resented by the Portuguese settlers at Luanda, who had already begun to suffer economically from Dutch competition. The long tension between the Portuguese in Angola and the *Mani*

Kongo became deeper, as the Kongolese monarch cleverly used Dutch traders, his Vatican mission, and his contacts with friendly Portuguese and Spanish priests to lessen the influence of Portuguese Angola in central Africa.

This complicated international situation, interwoven with the greed of both Europeans and Africans eager for the soaring profits of the slave trade, took a heavy toll on the political health of the kingdom of Kongo. At the same time that the *Mani Kongo* was cementing an alliance with Holland or Ndongo against the Portuguese in Luanda, one of his vassal princes might be secretly conspiring with the Portuguese to evade his authority by shipping slaves without his knowledge or approval. As the years wore on, the complexity of intrigue by both Dutch and Portuguese grew more bewildering.

The situation within Kongo was made far worse by the confusion over the laws regulating succession to the throne. After Affonso I, it had been generally agreed that only the descendants of his two sons and one daughter were eligible to become *Mani Kongo*. But with the passing of generations, the number of Affonso's descendants increased to dozens, then to hundreds. The governors of the six great Kongolese provinces were appointed from the higher ranking *infantes,* as Affonso's descendants were called, as were the administrators of the many districts into which each of the provinces was divided.

By the early 1600's Portuguese titles were officially used by these successors of Affonso, so that there was a long and complex list of members of the noble family: princes, dukes, donnas, marquises, and knights. As the number of descendants multiplied, the bickering among various claimants to the throne and their supporters also grew. Alvare II seems to have been the last monarch who was able to rule the country in comparative peace. After his death in 1614 the records show a rising number of struggles marking the ascension to the throne of each new king, as well as periodic outbreaks of rebellion by rivals after the king had been crowned. In both the ascension to the throne and the subsequent rebellions the numerous trading agents of the Dutch and Portuguese were incessantly at work, eager to gain allies from whom they could buy more slaves. Indeed, the armed conflicts within the kingdom produced more slaves, so that the European slave traders tended to benefit no matter who won.

In 1641 a new period opened in Kongolese history, stemming the tide of disorder and internal conflict for a brief time. In that year Garcia II, the last of the great Kongo kings in the mold of Affonso and the two Alvares, ascended to the throne. In the same year a Dutch fleet occupied the Portuguese fortress and city of Luanda, sending its defenders fleeing into the interior of Angola. Also, a large contingent of Italian Capuchin missionaries arrived in São Salvador, at Garcia's request, to ex-

54

pand the lethargic missionary and education program still being pursued by the kings of Kongo.

Garcia was more successful in restoring order within Kongo than any of his predecessors since the time of Alvare II, more than thirty-five years before, although he was forced to accept the secession of the province of Soyo as an independent principate for several years. With Dutch help, Garcia managed to maintain order during the 1640's and 1650's, although rebellions threatened to erupt throughout his reign. His efforts to expand education and prosperity were only partly successful, however, because the kingdom was struck repeatedly by pestilence and famine. Locusts swept across many of the farmlands in 1642, 1643, 1654, and 1658, and an epidemic, believed to be of plague, resulted in the deaths of nearly half the population in the years 1655–57.

Despite locusts, disease, famine, and internal rivalries Kongo reached a peak of power during Garcia's reign, and for the first few years of his successor, Antonio I, who came to the throne in 1661. Italian, Spanish, and Portuguese missionaries preached and built schools, so that the number of literate, Christian Kongolese was greater than ever before. Garcia made several attempts to curtail the slave trade, of which he wrote: ". . . instead of gold and silver and other goods which

55

function elsewhere as money, the trade and the money here are persons, who are not in gold, nor in cloth, but who are creatures. It is our disgrace and that of our predecessors that we, in our simplicity, have given the opportunity to do many evils in our realm. . . ."

The Dutch occupation of Luanda in 1641 was welcomed by Garcia and the kings of most African states in central Africa, who had little cause to love the Portuguese. Both Kongo and Matamba, the powerful state in the interior, formed alliances with the Dutch to fight against the Portuguese in other parts of Angola and won a number of victories over the Portuguese forces. But in 1648 a Portuguese fleet from Brazil forced the Dutch commander of Luanda to surrender, following which the Dutch withdrew, leaving their African allies to fight alone.

For the next few years the Portuguese in Angola concentrated their efforts on defeating Matamba, which was at the time ruled by the remarkable Queen Nzinga. Nzinga was from Ndongo, and had been queen of that state until she was driven out of Angola by the Portuguese. Settling in Matamba, she married into its royal family, accumulated a formidable army of Ndongo, Matamba, and Jaga, and continued the war against her Portuguese enemies. In 1656 she was finally defeated, and forced to sign a treaty by which she surrendered her rights to the throne of Ndongo and her lands in Portuguese Angola. With Nzinga eliminated as a serious threat, the aggressive Portuguese in Luanda turned their attention toward Kongo.

Between 1658, when Luanda mobilized a large army, and 1665 Luanda's agents developed a campaign of subversion and intrigue against Garcia II and his successor, Antonio I. In 1664 two Kongolese territories, Wandu and Ambwilu, were persuaded to renounce their allegiance to Antonio and accept the sovereignty of Portugal, and war ensued. In 1665 Antonio I was killed in battle, just as his army was inflicting a defeat on the Portuguese.

Following Antonio's death civil war broke out in Kongo, as rival factions battled to claim the throne. The Portuguese were fearful of intervening after their bruising contact with the Kongo army in 1665, but finally, in 1670, they sent an army into Kongo. The army entered the province of Soyo, where it was almost totally annihilated by the count of Soyo. This defeat ended the threat of Portuguese invasion of the Kongo heartland, but by this time there was little need for outright Portuguese conquest; Kongo had ceased to be a unified power.

Between 1665 and 1710 there was constant civil strife in Kongo, as rival kings based in Soyo, Mbamba, and Mpangu ruled parts of the kingdom and disputed the legitimacy of the others. Battles were frequent, although no force was strong enough to subdue the others and reunify the country. To make the unhappy situation worse, the growing numbers of *infantes*, with their Portuguese titles, began competing for rulership of the provinces, then of the districts within the provinces.

In 1710 one *Mani Kongo*, Pedro IV, succeeded in eliminating rival claimants to the throne, but by this time Soyo had become completely independent of the kingdom and most of the provinces were wracked by conflict over leadership. From

57

1710 on, until the end of the nineteenth century
when modern colonial rule was proclaimed over
all of central Africa, Kongo existed in a condition
which has often been compared with that of the
Holy Roman Empire in Europe during the Dark
Ages. The idea of a national king existed, and was
accepted by the people of the nation. This idea
served as a cultural bond, keeping alive a spirit of
kinship and common custom. But no strong king
appeared, able to raise an army, subdue rivals, and
rebuild the national government.

The glory and the promise of Affonso's Kongo,
and its pathetic struggles and gradual dissolution
after the 1650's, make a poignant story. A great
African kingdom, united under a ruler of grandeur
and vision, shone forth from the heart of central
Africa as a revelation to Europe and as a symbol of
the achievement of the Bantu civilization. Under
Affonso and his successors, for a century and a half,
a determined campaign was carried on by a number of worthy monarchs to utilize Christianity to
educate the people, develop prosperity, and mod-
ernize the land. But their great effort, inspired by
Affonso's dream, failed. It was a victim of many
forces. The Portuguese and Kongolese alike, hun-
gering for the wealth and power they could gain
from the evil slave trade, battled ceaselessly against
the forces of unity and progress led by the best of
the *Mani Kongo*s and their few Portuguese
supporters.

In the end the land was devastated by the ravages of the slave trade and the struggles for wealth
and power, and by pestilence and famine. Slowly
the kingdom deteriorated into a country of bicker-

58

ing princes, then into a host of tiny chiefdoms, some with fewer than a thousand people, each led by one of the numerous *infantes* who pretended to royalty because he was descended from Affonso.

Today the Kongo people still remember Affonso and the ancient days of glory with pride. Many still long for a new leader who can bring them together into a modern nation and resurrect the luster of the past. But history has made such a resurrection virtually impossible. There is no longer a pretender to the throne. The Kongolese people are divided among three modern states: the People's Republic of the Congo, with its capital at Brazzaville; the republic of Zaire, with its capital at Kinshasa; and the Portuguese colony of Angola, ruled from Luanda, where the Portuguese still cling to the foothold they first established in the sixteenth century. Yet the memory of the ancient past remains alive in the hearts of the Kongolese people, giving them a pride in their culture and in the achievements of their illustrious ancestors.

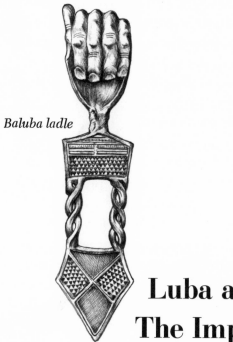

Baluba ladle

4

Luba and Lunda: The Imperial Idea

Far to the east of Kongo, nearly a thousand miles into the interior of central Africa, lies the country of the Luba peoples. Spread out around the Luba are large groups of closely related Lunda peoples, the two together covering an area of more than six hundred miles from east to west and four hundred miles from north to south. On the eastern rim of the Luba-Lunda country is the region of lakes where both the Congo and Zambezi rivers originate. This was the cradleland, covering the Zaire province of Katanga and adjacent Zambia, in which the earliest Bantu-speaking ancestors settled, and from which they sent out new settlers to populate all of central and southern Africa.

The territories inhabited by the Luba and Lunda

are part of the vast savanna which stretches more than fifteen hundred miles across the African continent, between the Atlantic and Indian oceans, from the coasts of Zaire and Angola to those of Mozambique and Tanzania. It is moderately dry country, with a rainfall that averages between thirty and forty inches per year. Much of the rain falls between October and February; the rest of the year has so little rain that much of the soil dries out, becoming parched and hard. There are forests of moderately tall trees whose leaves fall during the dry season, and most of the land is covered by wild grasses more than a foot high. The central African savanna resembles part of the American Midwest, with its great plains and prairies, although the soil is drier and poorer in Africa.

The savanna is not rich agricultural country, although its peoples live by farming. They use the same methods of cultivation as the Kongolese and grow much the same crops. Once great herds of game roamed the savannas and provided an abundant source of food for the hunters who lived there before the land was settled by the Bantu-speaking farmers. Today each Bantu community has a few hunters who go out to seek antelope, wart hog, small deer, and other game, but the vast herds have thinned out drastically in the face of human competition.

*Kata Mbula,
109th king of
the Bakuba,
1800–1810*

The heartland of Luba-Lunda country is laced by numerous rivers, especially those which flow north and west to form the massive Congo River. These smaller rivers and streams, which often flow through lakes and swamplands, provide better soil and water supplies than the surrounding savan-

61

nas. Most are rich with fish, which the people catch to enrich their diet. Some of the rivers and lakes have created fertile flood plains, on which the Luba and Lunda have built larger settlements and live a more prosperous life than the savannas themselves can support.

Luba-Lunda country has not been as thoroughly studied as some other parts of Bantu Africa, either by archeologists or by scholars who analyze African oral histories. Europeans had little contact with the region until the nineteenth century, so that there are few written records of earlier history. Nothing exists to tell of the dramatic highlights of the past that have been so well recorded for Kongo, by both European and African scribes.

Yet the kingdoms and empires created by the Luba and Lunda have had extensive influence throughout central Africa. From their lands came both people and ideas, for many centuries, to shape the better-known histories of other Bantu-speaking peoples over a vast area. Luba and Lunda developments between 1600 and 1900 are known to have had such wide influence that it is impossible to understand the affairs of modern Angola, Zaire, and Zambia without some knowledge of the Luba and Lunda, and their relations with their neighbors.

Very little is known of either people before about 1500. After 1600 a history can be sketched out in broad outline, by piecing together what is known from oral histories, legends, and the records of the few Europeans who visited after the eighteenth century. About the more distant past, however, only the great archeological find at Lake Kisale has provided both information and tantalizing questions.

Lake Kisale is a small lake around which live Luba peoples, in Zaire's Katanga province. Along its shores there are burial sites, marked by seemingly endless low mounds, which have been dated at about A.D. 700–800. Stretching for more than ten miles, the graves are so numerous that they have never been counted. It is estimated that there may be several hundred thousand graves in this vast cemetery, representing at least two or three centuries of burials by the peoples who lived around Lake Kisale. Whether the peoples who buried their dead in the cemetery are the ancestors of the Luba is not known. There are differences in styles of making pottery, for example, which suggest that the Luba may have migrated into the Lake Kisale area and absorbed the earlier settlers. Yet the Luba seem to have originated in the Katanga region, not far from Lake Kisale, and must have been related to the early Lake Kisale peoples even if there were differences.

The graves in the Lake Kisale cemetery which have been opened reveal that the people buried

there were far from poor or primitive. Most skeletons are ornamented with bracelets, bangles, and other jewelry of copper, gold, and iron, all of which are costly. In a few graves there have also been found decorative seashells from the Indian Ocean, which shows that the Kisale peoples had trade contacts with the peoples on the Indian Ocean coast, more than a thousand miles away. Most of the copper, gold, and iron, in fact, came from some distance away, since there are no known ores in the immediate vicinity of Lake Kisale.

The burial of these objects with the dead indicates the existence of a system of trade which covered considerable distances. Since there is no evidence that the graves are occupied by royalty, but only by ordinary people, it would seem that most Kisale people of each new generation were wealthy enough to accumulate expensive ornaments and jewelry that could be buried with them.

Just as important, however, is the fact that there are so many graves in a small area. The population along Kisale's shores must have been dense, for a long period of time. The soil must have been fertile; even today it is better than that in most of the central African savanna. And there must have been extensive fishing and hunting activity which brought into the towns of the lake large supplies of meat and fish to supplement the produce of the farmers.

The settlement of people in a dense pattern, obviously living in a fair state of prosperity, would also suggest that they had a centralized government which bound them together, maintained internal order, and protected them from invasion. There is, of course, no direct evidence of such a government; yet most peoples in Africa who are settled in the Kisale pattern have developed a centralized government, and virtually all the peoples of the Katanga area have had such governments for many centuries.

Unfortunately the civil wars and internal conflicts which plagued Zaire after it declared its independence from Belgium in 1960 have prevented archeologists from exploring the Kisale cemetery further or from making more extensive studies of the Katanga region. In a few years, when archeological study is resumed, many questions whose answers must now remain vague will undoubtedly be resolved.

What the Kisale finds indicate with little doubt, however, is that the area now inhabited by the Luba was settled by a prosperous, highly developed people more than a thousand years ago. Whether they were themselves Luba, or whether the Luba settled among them at a later time, the Luba clearly had a base of great cultural achievement upon which to build the rich kingdoms that appeared after about 1400.

Baluba figure

The founding of the greatest of the Luba states, Luba Kalanga, is dated at about 1500, but it was by no means the first Luba kingdom. Well before 1500 the whole Luba-Lunda country, like that around Kongo, was covered by scores of small kingdoms and chiefdoms, and at least two other Luba kingdoms were in existence when Luba Kalanga was founded.

The founding of Luba Kalanga, however, was an event of special significance for both the Luba peoples and their neighbors. From Luba Kalanga armies of conquest moved out after 1500, conquering surrounding chiefdoms and incorporating them into a large kingdom, really a small empire, that was different from the small states that had previously evolved in the area.

Before 1500 the Luba peoples were settled in a large area between Lake Kisale and other lakes of Katanga and the Bushimai River. To the west lived the Bungo, who were the ancestors of the Lunda, and who were closely related in language and culture to the Luba. To the east, between the Katanga lakes and Lake Tanganyika, lived the ancestors of the Hemba and Bemba peoples; the latter today form one of the most important ethnic groups in Zambia. The peoples to the east seem to have been living in small villages, ruled only by village chiefs, while those to the west were moving more rapidly toward states in which a number of villages came together under the rule of a chief or king. This was true of the Luba themselves. The Luba Kaniok and Luba Kalundwe had already, before 1500, developed states in which a number of chiefdoms had pledged allegiance to one king. The Luba Kalanga, like the Hemba and Bemba to their east, were grouped into a number of petty chiefdoms until 1500.

In 1500 the greatest Luba culture hero, a warrior named Kongolo, arrived in the country. He was a Luba, but his origin is disputed. Some traditions say that he came from Luba Kalundwe, from the northwest, while others say that he came from a land to the northeast, near the site of the modern town of Kongolo in present-day Zaire. When Kongolo arrived—according to legend he was an unusually brave and commanding personage—he subdued a number of chiefdoms and villages, organized a government over them, and built a capital at a small village named Mwibele. By uniting a number of Luba Kalanga chiefdoms he created a new Luba state that resembled those of Kaniok and Kalundwe.

A few years after Kongolo was proclaimed king, a second man of great importance to Luba history arrived, this time from a small state to the east. This visitor, a distinguished hunter named Ilunga Mbili, was of noble blood, and he married two of Kongolo's half sisters. (Polygamy was common in Bantu society. A man was considered wealthy if he married several wives, because they bore him many children; the wives and older children helped to till the fields and produce food.) Within a few months, however, Ilunga and Kongolo quarreled, because Ilunga insisted on trying to instruct Kongolo in the development of more civilized manners and more refined techniques of government. When Ilunga fled back to his own land, his two wives remained, and each bore a son.

Bakuba cup

67

One of the sons, Kalala Ilunga, grew up to be a brilliant soldier, who led contingents of Kongolo's army on campaigns to expand the territory of the kingdom. Kalala was so successful, and so popular among the Luba people, that Kongolo became jealous of his power and drove him into exile in the chiefdom of his father, Ilunga Mbili. There Kalala was well received, and he recruited an army which he led back into Kongolo's kingdom. Kongolo, by now an old man frightened of his nephew's power, fled, but was soon captured and executed. Kalala Ilunga then became king, building his own capital a few miles from Mwibele at Munza. Following his precedent, most later Luba kings built a new capital when they were crowned, allowing the previous capital to revert to a village.

The Luba national epic, which is still told by the old to the young around the fires at night, centers around the founding of the kingdom by Kongolo, the quarrels between Kongolo and Kalala Ilunga, and the triumphal seizure of the throne by the brilliant Kalala. Both men are revered as founding fathers, and the royal clans of all Luba kingdoms claim Kongolo as their ancestor.

Kalala went on to expand the kingdom by campaigning throughout his lifetime, conquering dozens of chiefdoms around his borders to build a great state, more powerful than any that had ever been created among the Luba. For nearly four centuries the Luba Kalanga state was considered the senior Luba kingdom, larger and more powerful than any other, although it never conquered the Luba states of Kaniok or Kalundwe.

The most important idea underlying the Luba

68

Kalanga kingdom was one introduced by Kongolo and strengthened by Kalala. Called *bulopwe* in the Luba language, it meant "rulership," but its importance lay in the fact that membership in the lineage of Kongolo and Kalala conferred *bulopwe* on the individual, and that any individual who possessed the quality of *bulopwe* was automatically of the ruling class, fit to stand above other men and rule them. All people who possessed this inherited power were called the *balopwe*.

In time the idea of *bulopwe* became a very powerful force in the growth and operation of the Luba kingdom. The Luba people accepted it and regarded the *balopwe* as rulers whose right to govern was by divine will. A well-organized government grew up, respected and obeyed by the Luba people.

In the Luba government the king, as the leader with the greatest *bulopwe*, was believed to have supernatural powers and consequently ruled with nearly absolute authority. His authority was limited in practice, however, by the fact that he had a number of brothers and half brothers who also possessed *bulopwe* and could rise against him if his rule became despotic and unpopular. To guard against plotting and rebellion by his kinsmen the king had to rule justly, and he had to share his power with his fellow *balopwe*. This he accomplished by appointing his powerful relatives to important government posts and by respecting their titles and positions.

The king ruled through a cabinet which consisted of the most senior *balopwe*. One minister was the head general, in charge of an officer corps which

Luba man

Ceremonial swords

served as a standing police force and as a nucleus for the army in time of war. Another, who headed the most important province in the kingdom, was the keeper of the sacred emblems of the royal lineage. Many of the governors of provinces spent part of their time at the capital, advising the king and serving in his cabinet. Taxes were levied by the king, and collected by the police corps. In outlying districts taxes were paid once a year, in the form of grain, animals, gold, copper, ivory, or oil, but in districts closer to the capital taxes were paid several times a year, frequently in grains and other foods to help feed the court and the numerous servants of the king.

The kingdom was divided into a number of provinces, each of which in turn was made up of a group of chiefdoms. The chiefdoms were composed of several villages, each with a small population. Some of the villages were ruled by hereditary chiefs who were not descended from Kongolo or Kalala and thus were not *balopwe,* while others were headed by chiefs appointed by the king or the governor, generally from among the *balopwe.* With the exception of hereditary chieftainships all offices in the kingdom were filled by the king's appointees, and he had the power to remove appointees if he was not satisfied with their performance.

The concept of *bulopwe* helped to lend strength to this structure of government, since so many of the administrators were possessed of its power and could claim descent from the founders of the kingdom. Within the Luba nation the system worked very well.

Outside the Luba peoples, however, the concept

70

of *bulopwe* had great limitations. Since a man could possess it only if he were a member of the Luba royal lineage, non-Luba chiefs and kings were automatically excluded. When the Luba king annexed a non-Luba chiefdom, he appointed a member of the *balopwe* to establish a camp near the capital of the new territory in order to supervise the collection of taxes and the performance of obligations to the king. Since this humiliated the local chiefs and kings, non-Luba peoples resisted incorporation into the Luba kingdom, and rebellions were frequent. Because of this limitation of the idea of *bulopwe*, the Luba kings were never able to build large empires which united Luba and non-Luba peoples under one government.

Ironically the concept of *bulopwe*, which served the Luba so well within their land but limited their ability to expand into a great empire, was eventually adopted by the Lunda and used to create a far-reaching imperial system. Between about 1600 and 1800 the concept of *bulopwe*, as used by the Lunda, helped to spread a system of well-organized government over a vast area of central Africa, stretching from what is now Tanzania to Angola and affecting the affairs of peoples in the areas now called Zaire, Zambia, Malawi, Mozambique, and Rhodesia.

The process of political development which helped to build the Luba kingdoms between about 1400 and 1550 was accompanied by a long period of migrations away from the Luba territory and the country around it. These migrations were generally movements of small numbers of people rather than extensive movements of large numbers. A chief of a

71

village or his sons might become ambitious to build up more power and wealth but would find that other chiefs in neighboring villages were too strong to permit expansion. The ambitious man, together with a few dozen or a hundred or so followers, would move to territory farther away where there were no chiefs or where the chiefs were weak. There he would settle, marrying one or more women of the local group's leading families, and establish himself as chief. His sons or brothers, in turn, might move a few years later in the same pattern, setting themselves up as rulers some miles away.

By this process the Jaga, who became a fierce and militaristic people, launched their invasions of the prosperous chiefdoms and kingdoms to the west, ravaging the territories of Kongo, Ndongo, Matamba, Kasanje, and other states. Although their origins are obscure, the Jaga seem to be related to the Luba and the Lunda, perhaps having split off from these groups between 1400 and 1500 and developing a different, more military way of life as they migrated to the west.

In the same process Luba members of the *balopwe* moved among the Lunda and their ancestors, the Bungo, conquering local chiefs and settling down to form small new states. The Luba conquerors, however, were absorbed by the Lunda, along with their concept of *bulopwe*, and the new lineages of Luba-Lunda royalty gradually abandoned the notion that *bulopwe* could be possessed only by descendants of Kongolo or Kalala. They retained the idea of *bulopwe* as a sacred force of leadership but gradually came to believe that it

Baluba figure

72

could be conferred by a *balopwe* king upon vassals who were not related to him by blood.

This new concept of *bulopwe* proved to have great importance. When a Lunda chieftain conquered a rival chieftain, or when the latter submitted to the Lunda without war, the new vassal could be granted "Lundahood" and continue to govern as he always had, but with even more prestige and power than before. He was required to pay taxes and tribute to the Lunda king, and to provide troops in time of war and workers for building roads. But the burden of these obligations was usually light, and the chief was able to continue his traditional role while sharing the authority of the Lunda ruling class.

The Lunda were able to adopt and extend this new concept of power because of their own flexible system of government, which had developed long before Luba influence. The basic unit in the Lunda system of government was the local village, headed by a chief whose position stemmed from his membership in the local ruling lineage. He was called "owner of the land," and presided over the allocation of farming plots as well as over disputes and religious ceremonies. Because his position was hereditary, the Lunda kings rarely attempted to replace him unless he was guilty of serious disloyalty. He paid taxes to the king, generally in the form of food, but otherwise governed his village as he saw fit. As the result of migrations over a period of several centuries the numerous Lunda village chiefs were generally related to each other, and they recognized their mutual kinship.

The Lunda king's government, like that of the

Luba, was represented in the villages or districts by an official whom he appointed. But these representatives were not considered rulers of the local areas, and they lived on lands given to them by the village chieftains. Their main function was to collect taxes and to arbitrate, on behalf of the king, when disputes over the chieftainship arose. In the royal capital, which was a large town with as many as fifteen thousand people, there were numerous noblemen and councilors, and local officials traveled there for council meetings and audiences with the king.

Well before Luba invaders entered Lundaland and brought the concept of *bulopwe,* the Lunda had organized a loosely knit kingdom on these lines, with a relationship of mutual obligation between the king and the "owners of the land." The invading Luba *balopwe* married into the Lunda aristocracy and were quickly absorbed into it; only the Luba titles brought by the *balopwe* remained to show the entry of Luba into the Lunda kingdom.

The Luba influence on Lundaland seems to have reached its peak between 1500 and 1600. After 1600 the Lunda kingdom began to expand, using some Luba ideas, and from this date the names of kings are known. The two most famous were Luseeng and his son Yaav Naweej, who ruled successively from about 1600 to 1650 or 1675. In the Lunda language the word *mwaant* means "chief" or "ruler," and it was used as a title for the Lunda kings. Luseeng is thus referred to as Mwaant Luseeng, and Naweej as Mwaant Yaav Naweej. Under Luseeng's reign the Lunda kingdom began to expand its territory gradually, incorporating a num-

Ornamented weapons

74

ber of non-Lunda chiefdoms and becoming a small, loosely knit empire. Mwaant Yaav Naweej continued his father's policy of expansion, so that by his death, sometime between 1650 and 1675, Lunda had become an extensive empire whose territory was already larger than any of the Luba kingdoms. And it was destined to grow larger still over the next two centuries, as it expanded both east and west to incorporate more and more peoples into the Lunda political and cultural system.

These two Lunda kings were so respected by the Lunda people that the throne came to be identified with them. After the death of Mwaant Yaav Naweej all later kings were titled *Mwaant Yaav*, which literally translated means "lord of the viper." Both Africans in other parts of central Africa and the Portuguese were familiar with the great Lunda kings in the deep heart of the continent, and the Portuguese believed the whole of central Africa to be part of the empire of the *Mwata Yamvo*, as he was known to them.

As the Lunda empire expanded, not all surrounding peoples were willing to accept its authority. Some resisted but were conquered over a period of time. Other groups, both large and small, seeking power and cultural freedom, migrated, frequently taking with them Luba and Lunda concepts of government. By this process many other great kingdoms that arose in central Africa between 1700 and 1900 were influenced by the Luba-Lunda tradition, and the modern descendants of their inhabitants trace their origins back to these contacts. Several of the most notable of these states are those of the Bemba of northern Zambia, the Lozi of southern Zambia, the Chokwe and the Lwena of southern Zaire and northern Angola, the Kasanje of Angola, and various states of the Maravi peoples of Malawi, Zambia, and Rhodesia.

In many of these states Lunda chieftains arrived during the seventeenth century and gradually acquired power. The royal lines of the Bemba, Chokwe, and Lwena kingdoms, for example, today trace their ancestry to Lunda clans, and their myths of origin relate how Lunda royalty came among them to found their kingdoms by intermarrying with local families. Each of these peoples speaks a Bantu language that shows kinship with Luba and Lunda, indicating that at some time, many centuries ago, they may have had a common origin. Whatever their origin, it is clear that Lunda political ideas and influences played a great role in the establishment and growth of their kingdoms between about 1600 and 1800. Many of the chieftains on the borders of Lundaland acknowledged the sovereignty of the Lunda king, especially during the 1700–1850 period, when Lunda power was at its zenith.

Chokwe carving

One of the areas settled by migrating Lunda chieftains was the Luapula Valley, which today forms the border between Zaire and Zambia. There a fertile strip of land lies along both sides of the Luapula River, for about one hundred miles above the point where the river flows into Lake Mweru. The flood plains in the valley are interlaced with canals and streams, which are filled with water during the rainy season but which leave fertile plots as the water recedes. The waters of the flood plain, the river itself, and Lake Mweru are

76

rich with fish. For many centuries the peoples of the Luapula Valley and the Mweru shores have enjoyed an abundant life, and their territory has been more densely populated than that of their neighbors on the savanna. At least one small Lunda chiefdom was built among the Luapula peoples during the reign of Yaav Naweej, and it served as the nucleus that was later to make the Luapula Valley one of the greatest strongholds of Lunda power.

During the period when Lunda political ideas were expanding vigorously across central Africa, the Lunda kingdom itself was still in the process of development and was not a strong military power. Lunda ideas influenced other states in central Africa, not because they were based on a powerful home kingdom, but because they were flexible, useful ideas that could be applied to build kingships in any society. It was not until well after 1700 that the Lunda homeland became a great power that could spread its influence through military strength.

The century between 1700 and 1800 witnessed great growth of both Luba and Lunda power in central Africa. The Luba controlled a broad band of territory for several hundred miles from Lake Kisale to the west, while the Lunda ruled a much larger territory south of Lubaland. The Luba were not united into one kingdom. The central Luba kingdom of Luba Kalanga was by far the largest, but three other small, strong Luba kingdoms had maintained a stout independence: Kalundwe, Kaniok, and Kikonja, the latter a diminutive state situated around the shores of Lake Kisale. In its growth Kalanga had incorporated numerous Luba clans and chiefdoms, and had absorbed much of Kalundwe's territory without destroying the Kalundwe kingdom itself. Many other Luba peoples lived outside the four kingdoms, in loosely organized chiefdoms east of Lake Kisale and west of Kaniok.

The original Lunda kingdom had gradually expanded into an empire. From their capital city of Musumba the *Mwaant Yaavs* ruled a vast land that stretched for hundreds of miles in every direction; in it were many non-Lunda chiefdoms as well as those of the Lunda themselves. The empire was growing; it did not reach its greatest size until after 1800. And far beyond the borders of the Lunda empire the influence of Luba-Lunda political ideas was reflected in dozens of states inhabited by other Bantu-speaking peoples.

Ceremonial mask

Between 1700 and 1800 the Lunda extended their power deep into the territories east of the capital, between the Lualaba and Luapula rivers and beyond. In this country there were many valuable salt deposits and copper mines, most of them controlled by Luba chiefs and chiefs of other non-Lunda peoples. As the Lunda expanded into this rich eastern region, conquering and absorbing the peoples already there, they conferred Lunda-hood on many of the conquered chiefs who were willing to participate in the affairs of the Lunda

78

empire, and Lunda peoples came to settle in their lands. As the empire grew, and the eastern regions became more influential in its affairs, the *Mwaant Yaav* appointed the senior Lunda chief of the area as governor, giving him the title *Kazembe.* By this time these two powerful rulers were known all across Africa as the *Mwata Yamvo* and the *Mwata Kazembe,* and those names were also used to refer to their countries.

Between 1750 and 1800 the *Kazembe's* lands grew almost as extensive as those of the *Mwata Yamvo* himself, and he became increasingly power-ful. He acknowledged the sovereignty of the *Mwata Yamvo* and sent annual tribute to Musumba, the capital city. By 1800, however, it was clear that the *Kazembe* was virtually an emperor in his own right. His armies ranged over a huge territory east of the Lualaba River, quelling resistance by local chiefs and adding them to the Lunda government. The center of power in the eastern province moved gradually eastward, toward the fertile Luapula Valley and the shores of Lake Mweru, so that by 1800 most *Kazembes* established their capitals in the Luapula-Mweru area.

Ceremonial mask

The strength of the *Kazembe's* government was based on the wealth of the copper and salt pro-duced in its territory, and on the general productiv-ity of its people. But it received a new source of wealth and power between 1790 and 1800, when it established direct trade relations with the Portu-guese trading settlement at Tete, far up the Zam-bezi River in what is now Mozambique. Prior to this time all European goods entering the eastern Lunda province had come from Angola, via the

79

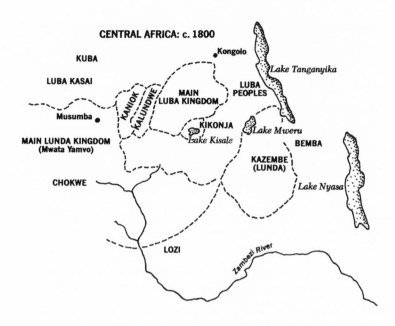

CENTRAL AFRICA: c. 1800

KUBA

LUBA KASAI

Musumba

MAIN LUNDA KINGDOM
(Mwata Yamvo)

CHOKWE

KANIOK

KALUNDWE

MAIN
LUBA KINGDOM

KIKONJA

Lake Kisale

Kongolo

Lake Tanganyika

LUBA
PEOPLES

Lake Mweru

KAZEMBE
(LUNDA)

BEMBA

Lake Nyasa

LOZI

Zambezi River

Lunda capital of Lusumba. After the 1790's the *Kazembe* had direct trade relations with the Portuguese in the other direction, toward the Indian Ocean, through lands over which the *Mwata Yamvo* had no control.

The great flexibility of the Lunda political system permitted the development of this two-headed empire. The *Mwata Yamvo* had no reason to fear the *Mwata Kazembe* so long as the latter sent annual tribute and continued to acknowledge the former as his master. The *Mwata Kazembe*, in turn, found that the payment of modest tribute and the acknowledgment of the *Mwata Yamvo's* seniority detracted little from his own wealth and power. By and large he was able to rule the eastern half of the empire as he chose, both feared and respected by his neighbors in other kingdoms and chiefdoms.

The two Lunda territories combined gave the Lunda political control over a vast land that stretched more than a thousand miles from east to west, and roughly five hundred miles from north to south.

Portuguese missions began to visit the country of Mwata Kazembe as early as 1798, after which accurate knowledge about the Lunda empire became available to Europe. In 1830–31 an expedition led by Major José Monteiro and Captain Antonio Gamitto visited the kingdom from Mozambique. Gamitto's account of this visit is important, because it provides the first written description of the Lunda empire and its achievements.

Gamitto found the *Kazembe*'s capital (located near the Luapula River at the time) to be "the greatest town in Central Africa," and noted that its streets were more than a mile long and were bordered by woven fences and living compounds, each containing a group of houses. In the great central square, where he was received by the *Kazembe*, he was impressed by the throngs of people, including a large part of the army, which he estimated to include five thousand to six thousand men.

The *Kazembe* himself Gamitto described as looking "fifty years old but we were told he is much older. He has a long beard, already turning gray. He is well built and tall, and has a robustness and agility which promises a long life; his look is agreeable and majestic, and his style splendid in its fashion." When the Portuguese were received, they found the *Kazembe* "seated on the left side of the eastern gate of the Musumba [which the court was called, after the central Lunda capital of the same

81

name]; many leopard skins served him as a carpet, the tails pointing outwards to form a star; over these was an enormous lion skin, and on this a stool covered with a big green cloth. On this throne the Mwata was seated, in greater elegance and state than any other *Mambo* ['king'] I have seen."

Gamitto was especially struck by the *Mwata Kazembe*'s royal regalia. His crown was covered with brilliant scarlet feathers; a diadem of beads of many colors and shapes wreathed his forehead; and his neck and chest were covered by necklaces of beads made of glass and cowry shells. Inserted in the beads were numerous small mirrors, which,

The Mwata Kazembe

when struck by the sun's rays, were too bright for one to look at directly.

The capital city and the surrounding countryside appeared abundant and prosperous to Gamitto —the markets filled with grains, vegetables, meat, fish, pottery, iron tools and weapons, cloth, and a variety of imported goods. By this time both the eastern and western Lunda kingdoms were actively engaged in a great trade system which spanned the African continent, connecting the Atlantic and Indian Ocean coasts. From Lundaland and its tributaries flowed a large quantity of ivory, gold, copper, tin, skins, feathers, grains, and slaves. Well before 1800 the Lunda had begun to participate in the booming slave trade, as their armies raided weaker chiefdoms all around their borders.

Just as the slave trade had contributed to the decline of the kingdom of Kongo between the late sixteenth and early eighteenth centuries, it eventually helped to destroy the two great Lunda empires of Mwata Yamvo and Mwata Kazembe. It will be necessary to digress slightly from the affairs of the Lunda themselves to describe the later history of the slave trade before it was finally abolished.

Britain, the United States, and most countries of Western Europe had outlawed the slave trade with Africa early in the nineteenth century. At that time, however, the demand for slaves in Brazil, Cuba, and Puerto Rico was enormous. The antislavery powers agreed to tolerate a continued slave trade in return for agreement by Brazil, Portugal, and Spain to operate only below the equator. By about 1810–1820 the center of the slave trade shifted southward. The areas that are now Angola, Zaire, Congo (Brazzaville), Mozambique, and Tanganyika soon became the major sources of slaves, and huge numbers were sold from these territories for the plantations of Brazil, Cuba, and Puerto Rico.

By 1850 antislavery forces in Europe were working energetically to outlaw the slave trade in the Southern Hemisphere as well, and by about 1870 the torrent of slaves being shipped to Latin America virtually dried up. But new markets for slaves had grown up, in Madagascar, Zanzibar, and Arabia. Numerous slave traders, based along the Indian Ocean coasts of Mozambique, Tanganyika, and Kenya, operated an extensive network stretching deep into central Africa. Between about 1850 and 1890 this network caused havoc among the Bantu-speaking peoples around Lakes Tanganyika and Malawi, and for hundreds of miles westward into Zaire. Both the Luba kingdoms and the two Lunda empires were affected by the frenzied search for slaves; often their rulers sold slaves to the traders from the coast, but on many occasions the traders organized armed expeditions which raided both kingdoms.

In 1862 a series of disputes over the succession to the throne arose in Kazembe, leading to internal strife which lasted for most of the next thirty years. Enterprising slave traders from western Tanganyika and Zambia added to the confusion by lending the support of their well-armed militia to one or another of the contending factions. By 1890, when both the slave raids and the tensions within the kingdom ended, Kazembe had shrunk to a small state covering only the lands along the lower Lua-

Barotse razor

pula River and the southern shores of Lake Mweru. At least 80 percent of its former territory had been lost, when strong chiefs asserted their independence during the time of troubles.

In 1890 the *Kazembe* was forced to accept British sovereignty over his territory east of the Luapula, and at about the same time the forces of Belgium's Leopold II, who ruled the Congo Free State at the time, declared the western lands of Kazembe to be part of the Congo.

After the 1860's a process of deterioration began in Mwata Yamvo as well, so that by about 1890 that empire had also dwindled to a small portion of its once vast territory. Ironically enough, Mwata Yamvo's troubles stemmed from the expansion of the Chokwe kingdom in northern Angola, which itself had been founded by Lunda immigrants and which had built a state modeled on the Lunda pattern of government. During the period 1880–1895, when Mwata Yamvo was at a low ebb of its fortunes, it was absorbed into the Congo Free State by Leopold's troops, and its career as an independent kingdom ended.

In the end the upheavals in central Africa caused by the slave trade helped to weaken all the great states of the Luba and Lunda peoples, just as it had in the case of Kongo much earlier. And like the Kongo, both the Luba and the Lunda never succeeded in finding a permanent solution to the problem of succession to the throne. In their countries a number of contenders had legitimate rights to the throne, and often fought against each other to gain it when the old king died. When there were no difficulties with outside forces, these conflicts

85

were eventually resolved, and the succession usually brought about the reunification of the kingdom. And, if the new king were a man of great ability, he was often able to expand the state and lead it to new peaks of power and splendor. When outside danger threatened, however, the conflicts during the interregnum allowed easy exploitation by enemies, and that is why the slave-trade period was one in which external enemies were numerous.

Another weakness of the Luba-Lunda political system lay in the fact that it rarely established a tightly knit pattern of royal control over the entire territory. The outlying districts and chiefdoms paid tribute once a year, but they were not closely supervised from the capital. When the king was harsh and unpopular, these farther-removed chiefdoms readily defected to other kingdoms. As the slave trade increased between 1850 and 1880, and both Luba and Lunda kings sold many of the subjects of outlying chiefdoms into slavery, defections became ever more frequent.

This weakness was ironic, since the great strength of the Lunda had originally been the flexibility with which they absorbed chiefs into their own ruling class, giving them an honorable position in the Lunda kingdom. But after long periods of time, the Lunda kings often found themselves overextended. Their power to discipline chiefs far away from the capital was limited by the great size of the territory being ruled and the relatively small size of the king's armies.

For the same reasons the central government was often powerless to protect the outlying chiefdoms. During the nineteenth century these areas were sometimes raided with impunity by neighboring peoples participating in the slave trade. The kings of both the Luba and the Lunda, in fact, sometimes cooperated with slavers by allowing them to raid chiefdoms far from the capital, especially those that had been slow to pay tribute or had seemed troublesome. The result was that these distant chiefs had to fend for themselves. Some became slavers themselves. Others joined neighboring kingdoms (such as the Chokwe) which they felt might protect them. Still others banded together into new, smaller kingdoms for mutual defense. The process rapidly eroded the size and power of the Luba and Lunda kingdoms, especially those of the Lunda. By the period 1880–1890, when the colonial conquest by Belgians, Portuguese, British, and Germans began, they were in their weakest condition. By 1900 all had been absorbed into one or another of the European colonies of central Africa.

The imperial idea which originated in Lubaland and was spread by the Lunda so widely across central Africa helped to shape the history of the area from 1500 to nearly 1900. In the end, however, it proved incapable of protecting the peoples who adopted it against the ravages of the slave trade and the European conquest.

The Acropolis,
Zimbabwe

5

Zimbabwe: Mysterious
Relics of Glory

The great kingdoms created by Bantu-speaking peoples in Kongo, Luba, Lunda, and other parts of the central African savanna left few signs of their notable achievement, except in the legends of their people and in a few scattered manuscripts. Even the outstanding sculptures that their artists are believed to have made were carved in wood and have long since crumbled to dust under the attacks of insects and bacteria. From time to time graves have yielded bits and pieces of jewelry of copper, gold, and iron, and fragments of finely made pottery. But in the whole vast region, no great monuments of stone or mortar have been found, because the creative energies of the people were never turned to architecture.

88

When European explorers and settlers penetrated the highlands of Rhodesia and Zambia, however, they began to find the ruins of long-aban-
doned buildings and enclosures. Their exteriors
crumbling and their interiors ransacked, these great
structures had clearly been built by a civilized people who had mastered the use of stone for building
and art. Virtually all Europeans who entered
the region dismissed the notion that the Bantu-
speaking inhabitants could have built such impos-
ing edifices.

The attention of the European visitors and of
scholars in much of the world centered on the
massive ruins at Great Zimbabwe, a site located
just off the modern highway between the Rhodesian cities of Salisbury and Fort Victoria. There a
space of more than sixty acres is covered with giant
walls, enclosing large oval areas, and an intricate
pattern of walkways, steps, alcoves of cut stone and
living rock, and carved stone statuary. Serving today as one of Rhodesia's most popular tourist at-
tractions, the Zimbabwe ruins are described by
most who see them as "mysterious," "brooding,"
"awesome," and "magnificent."

The world's attention was first called to the Zimbabwe ruins in 1868, when a German-American
hunter, Adam Renders, saw them while wandering
the central Rhodesia plains in search of big game.
Renders reported the ruins, obviously impressed,
but advanced no theory about their origin; he simply noted that they lay in the lands of the Shona
peoples (another group of the Bantu-speaking family), who built mainly in mud and straw. In 1872
a German geologist, Karl Mauch, visited Zimba-

bwe and reported that it could only have been built by a highly civilized people of the remote past, probably visitors to Africa who came to mine gold. As he studied the mystery—and collected some of the gold objects he found among the ruins—Mauch concluded that this must be the site of King Solomon's mines, from which the Israelites brought great quantities of gold to decorate Solomon's splendid temple and palace.

Zimbabwe's ruins are dominated by two vast structures. Covering the top of a granite hill is a series of walls and small enclosures, some of them perched on an eighty-foot cliff. Visible for many miles, the ruins on the hilltop are called the Acropolis; they do remind one somewhat of the great Greek Acropolis which stands so splendidly atop its hill in Athens. The Zimbabwe Acropolis, surrounded by thick walls and divided into a complex pattern of steps, small enclosures, alcoves, parapets, and platforms, seems to have served as a defensive bastion, protecting the inhabitants from marauding troops or wild animals. When manned by soldiers, it must have been impregnable. Inside its strong walls the people built houses, probably occupied by priests and royalty, though none of them still stand.

In the valley below, several hundred yards from the base of the Acropolis of Zimbabwe, lies the Great Enclosure, a massive wall seventeen feet thick at its base, and four feet to eleven feet thick at the top. Its circumference is more than 800 feet, enclosing a great ellipse some 300 feet long and 200 feet wide. Within the massive walls of the Great Enclosure people also built houses, and altars. On its southern side is the Conical Tower, a perfectly

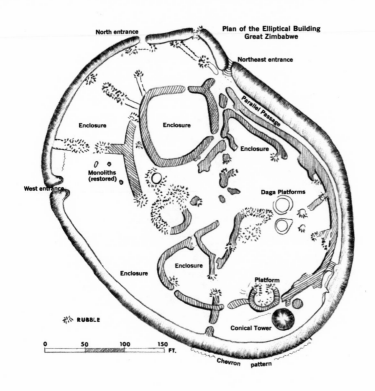

Plan of the Elliptical Building
Great Zimbabwe

North entrance

Northeast entrance

Parallel Passage

Enclosure

Enclosure

Enclosure

Monoliths
(restored)

West entrance

Daga Platforms

Enclosure

Enclosure

Platform

RUBBLE

0   50   100   150
FT.

Conical Tower

Chevron   pattern

The Great Enclosure

Conical Tower,
Zimbabwe

proportioned cone of stones some thirty-five feet
high, whose function is still unknown. Although the
walls of the Great Enclosure reveal masterful
stone-working skills, the Conical Tower is the most
impressive architectural achievement of the Zimbabwe ruins. Like many of the buildings at Zimbabwe,
it was built of rectangular stones that had been
carefully shaped and smoothed so that they would
fit together almost perfectly, with no lime or mortar to bind them.

Both the Temple, as the Great Enclosure is often
called, and the Acropolis were obviously built over
a period of several centuries, since the building
style varies greatly. The lower parts of the walls—
the first to have been built—were erected by stonemasons whose skills were not highly developed.
They selected stones that were not equal in size or

shape and piled them one on top of the other with no purpose but to produce a sturdy edifice. The upper parts, obviously built later by more skilled masons, were constructed with regularly shaped stones set in intricate patterns, the most common being that of the chevron. On one side of the Great Enclosure the chevron pattern is used for 168 feet, forming a beautiful design in the wall.

Stonework pattern, Great Enclosure

Curved steps, Great Enclosure

Statuary is believed to have decorated many alcoves and platforms in both the Temple and the Acropolis, though only a few beautifully sculptured birdlike figures, carved in soapstone, still remain. All the rest was either destroyed by invading troops during the nineteenth century or stolen by fortune hunters who pillaged Zimbabwe after Mauch popularized its existence.

Mauch, and many Europeans who followed him, were struck by the resemblance between the Zimbabwe structures and Biblical descriptions of ancient buildings of the Holy Land. Mauch theorized that the Zimbabwe Acropolis was a copy of King Solomon's temple atop Mount Moriah, and the Great Enclosure (or "elliptical building," as he called it) was a copy of the palace in which the Queen of Sheba is reported to have stayed when she visited King Solomon's court. There is a superficial resemblance to descriptions of these Biblical structures, but more systematic study shows that the buildings at Zimbabwe are distinctively African in style and purpose. The Great Enclosure, a magnificent achievement to be admired by the most gifted stonemason or architect, is clearly an elaborate, vast, and permanent enclosure built on the same pattern as the simple enclosures of stones or branches which most pastoral people of southern Africa erect to shelter their flocks at night.

A few years after the world learned of Zimbabwe, European explorers began to discover other sites, generally smaller but obviously built by the same ancient peoples, over a wide area of the Rhodesian plateau. By about 1900 more than a hundred such ruins had been located. Some consisted only of small enclosures, while others, such as those at Khami and Dhlo Dhlo in Rhodesia, were much larger and quite skillfully built, rivaling Zimbabwe in beauty if not in size.

Chevron and checker pattern, Dhlo Dhlo

In many of the ruins the early explorers found gold ornaments, as well as numerous objects of art in copper, stone, and clay. Since the Rhodesian plateau was laced with small gold mines, fortune hunters began to flock to the ancient stone sites to search for the gold and works of art that they contained. In 1895 one group even secured a concession from the British South Africa Company, which governed the area, to form an enterprise called The Ancient Ruins Company, Limited; its license granted it exclusive rights to exploit the ruins for

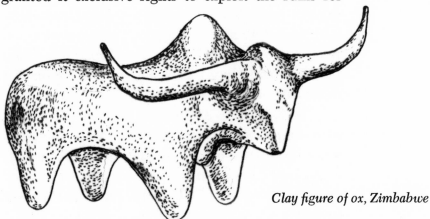

Clay figure of ox, Zimbabwe

whatever gold or art could be found. The concession was revoked in 1900, but by then The Ancient Ruins Company and dozens of individual adventurers had denuded many of the ruins of any
objects of value, leaving only the stone structures
and buried debris for archeologists to explore.

Further evidence of the richness and artistry of
the Bantu civilization on the Rhodesian plateau has
been revealed by one find which was not plundered.
Known as Mapungubwe, from the hill on which its
most important remains have been found, this site
clearly reveals that the peoples of the Rhodesian
plateau had developed a high material culture.

Mapungubwe is located near the juncture of the
Shashi and Limpopo rivers, in the Transvaal province of South Africa, not far from where modern
South Africa, Botswana, and Rhodesia adjoin each
other. It is roughly 200 miles southwest of Zimbabwe, and lies on the edge of the region of extensive
stone ruins. Long regarded by the local African
peoples as a sacred spot, Mapungubwe was not
explored until 1932 and afterward. The area in
which it is situated is relatively wild and thus not
densely inhabited, and has never attracted a large
European settlement. For many decades the Mapungubwe hill stood alone and brooding on the
plains, avoided by Africans and ignored by the few
Europeans who had seen it.

In 1932 a local Boer farmer named van Graan,
who supplemented his income from farming by
prospecting in the northern Transvaal, decided to
locate and explore Mapungubwe; the many references to it as a sacred hill, he reasoned, might mean
that its summit would yield ancient wealth. Even-

Soapstone figure,
Zimbabwe

tually van Graan found an African who was willing to show him how to scale the sheer sides of the hill, a secret most Africans either did not know or refused to reveal. Mapungubwe is some 200 feet high, almost vertical, and it is more than a thousand feet long. The top is level, so that the hill presents the appearance of a giant, flat-topped mound surrounded by plains. The only way to scale the sides, van Graan learned, was by way of a natural channel that runs from the hill's bottom to its top. In this channel the early inhabitants of the area had chiseled a series of holes in which they apparently anchored short logs to form a kind of ladder. Van Graan and his party, with some difficulty, reached the top by using the holes as resting places for their hands and feet as they climbed.

Mapungubwe's level top, van Graan found, was littered with thousands of fragments of pottery. After a day's searching, his party also found a small piece of worked gold, and they began to scratch in the soil to unearth more. In their first investigation they found more than seventy-five ounces of gold, all worked into thin plate, foil, tacks, and ornaments. Fortunately for our knowledge of the southern African past, van Graan's son reported the find to his former professor of history at the University of Pretoria, who persuaded the South African government to declare Mapungubwe a protected site; later van Graan and his companions surrendered the gold objects they had found to the university's museum.

Archeological investigations over the next few years showed that Mapungubwe was a remarkable find. The top was covered by tens of thousands of

tons of soil which had apparently been carried up, slowly and laboriously, in order that the chiefs and priests who resided on the summit could grow food. Numerous graves were found, and in them were skeletons richly adorned with jewelry and ornaments of gold, copper, and iron. In addition to bracelets and bangles archeologists found many finely wrought gold figurines of animals. Much of the pottery had been sheathed in thin gold foil. Other ornaments and figurines had been carved in wood, with gold foil then ingeniously tacked over the entire figure.

Rhinoceros of beaten gold, Mapungubwe

The plains around the foot of Mapungubwe have been excavated to a limited extent since 1932, although neither the plains nor the hill itself have been studied as extensively as historians wish. The evidence of the hilltop and the plains around it, however, makes it clear that the area was inhabited by a people who had evolved considerable skill in mining and metalworking. They used the hill as a sacred center where their priests and chiefs lived and were buried. The area shows continuous habitation since about the sixth or seventh century, and the pottery and other artifacts indicate that there

98

was continuing influence on the culture from other parts of the Rhodesian plateau. From about 1400 to 1500 on, the influence of the Shona peoples who built Zimbabwe is especially strong, suggesting that Mapungubwe was a western outpost of the Shona culture.

The entire Rhodesian region, which has been extensively settled by British colonists, was a major center of the Bantu civilization between about A.D. 400 and 1900, with its peak of development occurring between about 1400 and 1800. For the period up to 1400, all the evidence comes from archeologists, who have worked more extensively in Rhodesia than in most parts of Africa. After 1400 there is a great deal of information from both archeology and oral history, and Portuguese written accounts add valuable data after 1500. When put together, this evidence shows that Zimbabwe, Mapungubwe, and hundreds of other locations were all parts of one great cultural center.

The story begins, rather hazily, at about A.D. 100, with a site today called the Machili Forest Station. There archeologists have found signs of an ancient settlement. They have discovered fragments of pots, pieces of charcoal, and a piece of iron ore. The pottery and charcoal have been dated at somewhere between about 150 B.C. and A.D. 300; many authorities agree that A.D. 100 is as accurate an estimate as any other. The most significant thing about the Machili find is that the pottery is of a type made by many iron-using peoples at about that time and for many centuries later; the charcoal, of course, indicates that iron was smelted at or near the site. Machili thus provides the first evidence

99

that the African Iron Age had reached the southern African region; it is almost certain that the peoples who brought the knowledge of iron and the type of pottery found there were the ancestors of the Bantu-speaking peoples.

Machili Forest is located in the Zambezi River Valley, in the southeastern quadrant of modern Zambia, and is more than 500 miles northwest of Zimbabwe. But it is in the direction from which the Bantu-speaking peoples migrated as they spread out from their Katanga cradleland. Machili must represent one of their very earliest outposts in this migration.

The second part of the story begins a century or two later, between about A.D. 200 and 400, with the spread across a wide area of southern Africa of a culture which archeologists call Gokomere, from the village in Rhodesia where its pottery and other artifacts were first found. Gokomere is only a few miles from the Zimbabwe ruins, and Gokomere artifacts have been discovered deep down in excavations at Zimbabwe. The Gokomere people were apparently the dominant people on the entire Rhodesian plateau for many centuries, because their pottery and other relics have been found over an area that stretches more than 500 miles, from north of the Zambezi to south of the Limpopo, and an equal distance east and west between these two great rivers.

In the far east of Rhodesia, along the border with Mozambique, the plateau ascends steadily until it ends in a chain of mountains 5,000 to 6,000 feet high. In that broken country no evidence of the Gokomere culture has been found, but relics of a

similar culture, called Ziwa, indicate Gokomere influence on the pottery techniques of the mountain
people.

The Gokomere culture is easily recognized by
the pottery its people made. A large variety of

shapes were fashioned, ranging from large rounded
pots to flat bowls. Most had thick walls, and were
fired rather crudely so that their surfaces tended to
be somewhat rough. The necks and upper parts of
the vessels were usually decorated with stamped
or incised depressions, or channels made by lines
drawn in the wet clay, all in geometric designs. The
pots and bowls were not often colored, although
some were. They were stout, serviceable vessels,
but not of high technical or artistic quality.

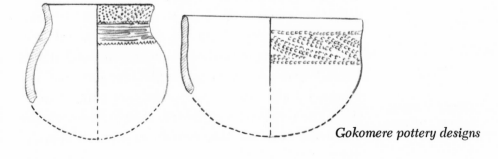

Gokomere pottery designs

The Gokomere people were farmers, cultivating the millet, beans, and other crops that have long been typical of central and southern Africa. They depended heavily on meat as well, herding goats, sheep, and probably cattle, as well as hunting the abundant wild game. This part of Africa is generally better suited to herding than to farming, although most areas will produce crops.

Most Gokomere sites have yielded no skeletons, because they decompose in the soils of southern Africa. Where skeletons have been found, however, they are of both Khoisan and Bantu racial types, even though Bantu speakers almost certainly were responsible for introducing the culture. Some Khoisan peoples apparently adopted the Gokomere ways of making pottery, and mining and smelting iron, and were eventually absorbed into the advancing Bantu communities.

Where the Gokomere culture originated is not known, although it was clearly brought into southern Africa by the ancestors of the Shona and other Bantu-speaking peoples who now live there. It represents the first definite expansion of the Bantu civilization into the region, and was accompanied by a well-developed knowledge of agriculture, improved techniques of house building, the potter's art, and above all, the technology of metallurgy —the knowledge of mining, smelting, and working iron and copper into a variety of useful tools and fine ornaments. By about A.D. 500–600 it had spread over the Rhodesian plateau and had developed local variations in the adjacent regions. The Ziwa culture of the Rhodesian-Mozambique highlands was one of the most extensive local varia-

Copper ingots used as currency, Rhodesian plateau

102

tions of Gokomere. The basic Gokomere pattern was the model from which most later cultures evolved in southern Africa, influencing the pottery, tool-making, economic techniques, and customs of the many peoples who continued to migrate into the region.

The Gokomere people inhabited the Zimbabwe site, but they did not possess either the knowledge of building in stone or the political and religious needs which made stone building so important to the later history of Zimbabwe.

In Zambia, itself dominated by a vast plateau north of the Zambezi River, other cultures somewhat similar to the Gokomere were developing at about the same time. And in western Rhodesia and adjacent Botswana and Transvaal still another basic culture, called the Leopard's Kopje culture, was at first influenced by Gokomere but soon developed its own distinctive styles of making and decorating pottery and tools. *Kopje* is the Dutch word for a small, flat-topped hill, and the Leopard's Kopje culture was that of the inhabitants of the area of Mapungubwe, some of whom were Khoisan peoples in the earlier periods of Mapungubwe settlement.

By A.D. 900–1000 an enormous region of southern Africa was populated by peoples of the Gokomere culture or cultures such as the Leopard's Kopje that paralleled it. Their movement toward the south continued; by 1000 they had reached deep into the Transvaal and Natal provinces of South Africa, Botswana, Swaziland, and Mozambique. Only the Cape Province of South Africa, southern and central Botswana, and Namibia were still inhabited by

103

Stone Age peoples, who knew nothing of the refined agricultural, pottery-making, and metallur-
gical skills of the expanding Bantu civilization.

By this same time a trade system had developed,
linking some of the Rhodesian and Zambian peoples
to the Indian Ocean, where a new trading empire,
controlled by Arabs and Bantu-speaking Africans,
had been established. Out of southern Africa
flowed a substantial quantity of ivory, gold, copper, iron, skins, feathers, and slaves, down the great
river valleys of the Zambezi, Limpopo, and smaller
rivers to commercial centers along the coasts of
Mozambique and Tanzania. From there the African
goods were carried by Arab ships (called dhows)

up the coast of East Africa to bustling markets in
Arabia, China, Persia, and India. In return a flow of
goods from these lands began to enter central and
southern Africa: fine cotton cloth, Indian iron tools
and weapons, delicate chinaware from India and
China, glass beads and bottles, polished shells, and
coins. In many early burial sites archeologists have

found evidence that these goods were beginning to trickle into the Rhodesian plateau by A.D. 1000, although they are much more abundant several centuries later.

The third part of the story of the rise of Bantu civilization on the Rhodesian plateau is the growth of this commercial system, and the most illustrative evidence comes from an archeological site at Ingombe Ilede, just north of the plateau near the great Kariba Gorge of the Zambezi, in modern Zambia. Here, in the Zambezi valley, a number of richly ornamented skeletons have been recovered from graves in a spot which seems to have been a center for elephant hunters. The Ingombe Ilede skeletons were buried clothed in fine cotton cloth, at least some of which was spun locally; a number of clay spindle whorls for spinning cotton have been found at the same site. Their arms and legs were sheathed in bangles of copper and gold, and a number of iron tools have been found nearby. Necklaces and belts of shells and gold, very artistically made, were strung around the necks and waists of several of the skeletons.

The Ingombe Ilede people were obviously wealthy, and they had a highly developed culture. The numerous fragments of pottery found in their graves and nearby are of excellent quality. Made in a variety of sizes and shapes, the pots were finely fired, often burnished to a lustrous polish with graphite, and occasionally colored. Brian Fagan, an archeologist who has studied the Ingombe Ilede burials, considers the pottery to be among the best ever produced in southern Africa.

The Ingombe Ilede artifacts date roughly to the

period A.D. 900–1200. The wealth of the people, and the numerous imported goods buried in the graves, show that they were involved in a lucrative trade system. It is believed that they may have been middlemen, trading ivory tusks, gold, and copper produced by other African peoples for cloth, shells, and beads from the Indian Ocean coast. But the importance of the Ingombe Ilede evidence is that it attests to the existence, by about A.D. 1000, of a trade system between the Zambia-Rhodesia area and the coasts of Mozambique and Tanzania.

The fourth part of the story is the gradual expansion into the Rhodesian area of the Shona peoples, one of the most extensive groups of Bantu speakers, who brought to the area a new, higher level of civilization after about A.D. 1000. They were responsible for the great ruins at Zimbabwe and so many other locations. The earliest Shona migrants must have begun to enter the area very early, for the topmost levels of the Ingombe Ilede site show definite Shona influence on the pottery of the people buried there, around A.D. 1000–1200.

The Shona are a numerous people, today inhabiting much of Rhodesia, Mozambique, and parts of South Africa, and many of the surrounding

106

peoples of Malawi and Zambia are related to them. The Shona language is divided into a number of dialects, each spoken by extensive clans that regard themselves as somewhat separate from the others, even though all acknowledge their Shona affiliation. One of the largest of these groups, and the one that made a deep imprint on the history of southern Africa, is the Karanga. Their precise origin is unknown, but both their oral traditions and their language suggest that they moved southward from the Katanga area during the first millennium, perhaps between A.D. 500 and 900, in a long, slow series of migrations. By A.D. 1000 their ancestors had crossed the Zambezi River and were settling among the earlier inhabitants of the Rhodesian plateau.

The influence of the Karanga is shown in the archeological investigations at Zimbabwe itself. The earliest Iron Age settlers of Zimbabwe were the Gokomere people, but they abandoned their settlement there by about A.D. 400. Around 600 to 700 a different people, whose pottery and artifacts show some slight resemblance to the Leopard's Kopje culture, established a village at Zimbabwe, and from that time on the site was continuously occupied. About 1000 to 1100, however, the culture began to change, under the influence of new immigrants who settled among the established peoples. The changes that began by 1100 seem to have stemmed from early Karanga influences; the pottery styles show definite similarity to later pottery known to have been made by Karanga peoples.

For nearly four centuries Zimbabwe experienced the development of a new cultural style. The qual-

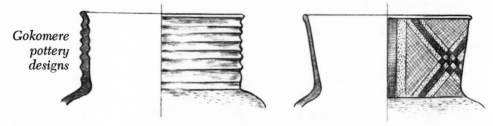

Gokomere pottery designs

ity of the pottery improved, showing better knowledge of firing and polishing techniques and more elaborate decoration of pots and bowls. The number and variety of tools and weapons of iron increased, and many foreign goods began to appear in the area. Houses grew larger and were much sturdier than those of earlier periods. Earthen platforms were carefully prepared, then foundations of stone were erected around the platforms. On the foundations the people erected a framework of poles, which they plastered with *daga,* a building material of earth and water, somewhat like adobe, which hardened in the sun. The walls of the new type of house were thicker and more durable than the earlier type, and verandas were often constructed in front of the houses.

The Karanga immigrants seem to have filtered into the area over a period of a century or more and to have gradually established themselves as a ruling class. Their great interest was in controlling the trade in precious metals, and they seem to have organized the local inhabitants in order to expand their mining industry. Karanga peoples had by this time become the dominant population along the Zambezi valley adjacent to the northern rim of the Rhodesian plateau, near the modern towns of Sena and Tete. There they were in contact with the Arab and Swahili traders who sailed up and down the coasts of eastern Africa, and who in turn sold

African goods to the great ships of Arabia, Persia, India, and China that plied the Indian Ocean.

Under the Karanga overlords Zimbabwe began to prosper as a center of government and religion. Its unique location made it ideal as a capital and religious center. Although located in a comparatively dry part of the plateau, where there are few deposits of gold or copper, Zimbabwe remains green and moist for most of the year. Moisture-bearing breezes from the Indian Ocean blow toward it in the channel of the Mtelikwe valley, bringing frequent mists and rains. It thus is a kind of oasis, favorable for growing crops, and has long been regarded as a blessed spot for this reason.

The Karanga introduced a religion to the Rhodesian plateau which enabled them to strengthen their political power, especially when they controlled favored locations such as Zimbabwe. In their religion there is one supreme God, called Mwari, who created man and the universe, and whose good will is essential if man's life is to be happy and prosperous. They preached that the most effective way to secure Mwari's blessing was through community worship, in which the entire community prayed through their leaders to Mwari for good rains and crops. Once established in Zimbabwe, the Karanga rulers were able to convince the people that their prayers brought rain and prosperity, at least in that location. Over a long period of time the Karanga chiefs came to be accepted as religious as well as political and economic leaders, and they were believed to have special access to Mwari.

Iron gongs, Rhodesian plateau

Once the Karanga system was established at Zim-

109

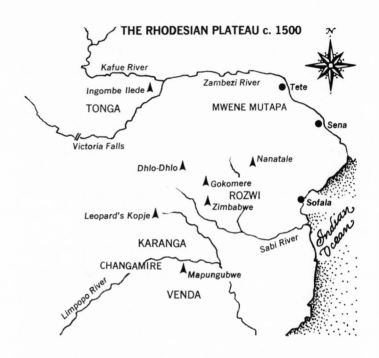

Kafue River

Ingombe Ilede ●   Zambezi River ● Tete

TONGA   MWENE MUTAPA

● Sena

Victoria Falls

Dhlo-Dhlo ▲   ▲ Nanatale

▲ Gokomere

ROZWI

▲ Zimbabwe   ● Sofala

Leopard's Kopje ▲

KARANGA   Sabi River

Indian Ocean

CHANGAMIRE ▲

Mapungubwe

Limpopo River   VENDA

babwe the first structures of stone were built on the Acropolis. Between 1100 and 1400 massive stone walls were erected on top of the Acropolis hill, connecting huge natural boulders that lie around the edges of the hill. One end of the hill was developed as a center of religious ceremony, while the other served as the residence of the chiefs and their entourage.

By 1400 the Karanga had covered much of the Rhodesian plateau, and the earlier inhabitants had been absorbed. About this time another Shona clan, the Rozwi, began to develop power in the north of the country, and they soon established themselves as the ruling class, over the Karanga, much as the Karanga had done several centuries earlier. And with the advent of the Rozwi a true history of the Rhodesian plateau begins, for their oral his-

tories provide the names and achievements of kings
from about 1400 on into modern times.

The next part of the story of Bantu civilization
in Rhodesia is concerned with the way in which
the Karanga and Rozwi built up a formidable empire, which eventually became one of the most
illustrious achievements of the Bantu-speaking
peoples.

Between about 1100 and 1300 the main theme
of Rhodesian history was the spread of the Karanga
people over the plateau, and the establishment of
their culture, their control of mining and trade, and
a confederation bound together by their ruling
clans. By 1300, if not earlier, two outside forces
began to influence the Karanga, making it desirable for them to develop a military system and a
stronger central government.

The first of these forces was the constantly growing commercial system which linked much of central and southern Africa with the thriving maritime
trade of the Indian Ocean. As the flow of goods in
and out of Africa grew, the Karanga rulers had to
build up a police force which would protect their
control of the trade and safeguard the wealth and
position of their nobles.

The second force was the threat of invasions
from the west. From that direction the great Kalahari Desert was slowly expanding—as it still is today
in modern Botswana—drying out the grasslands
that border it on the east. As the desert enlarged,
the peoples living around it tended to move toward
the more fertile east, where the Karanga nation
had established itself. To prevent them from over-
running the country, the Karanga needed a mili-

111

tary force. By 1300 the pressure of population from northern Botswana was substantial, and there is believed to have been continuing conflict between the Karanga and the Botswana herders and farmers.

Soapstone monolith, Dhlo Dhlo

During these times of encroachment and conflict, the Karanga people increasingly used their skill in stone building to erect defensive centers. From the archeological investigations of Zimbabwe, Khami, Dhlo Dhlo, and many other stone ruins it is clear that the construction of enclosing walls began during the Karanga period, as early as 1100 in the east and several centuries later in the west. The basic plan of the stone structures is the enclosure, which served to protect both people and their herds at night against wild predators, and into which they could retreat in case of attack from a strong party of warriors. Over a period of centuries the enclosures became larger and more elaborate, and by 1400 there was a great amount of building for religious purposes as well.

At least by 1400 the Rozwi clan had established a kingdom on the northern part of the Rhodesian plateau, near the Zambezi River. The extent of its territory at that time is not known, but it must have exercised great influence over most of the Karanga nation. Probably dozens of lesser Karanga chiefs sent tribute to the *Mambo*, as the king was called.

In about 1440 a great Rozwi king, Mutota I, began a campaign of conquest to consolidate the Karanga nation firmly under his control. At this time his capital was located some distance south of the Zambezi, probably near the Sabi River, which served as a commercial route to the coast. Near

112

the mouth of the Sabi lay the settlement of Sofala, the main concentration point for the trade between inner Africa and the Indian Ocean. Mutota's objective was to build a strongly united kingdom which would stretch from the Indian Ocean, with its trade routes converging on Sofala, inland as far as the Karanga nation had settled, nearly as far as the Kalahari Desert. Had he succeeded, this would have given him command of an empire roughly 700 miles from east to west and 500 miles from north to south. His north-south objectives seem to have been all the territory between the Zambezi and Limpopo rivers.

Mutota had the full support of his Rozwi kinsmen, as well as the advice and financial support of the numerous Swahili commercial agents. There were as many as 10,000 Swahili traders in the Rozwi kingdom at the time, working in close alliance with Mutota and other Rozwi leaders to further the lucrative trade with the Indian Ocean.

These Swahili traders will become much better known to the reader in a later chapter, but it is helpful to identify them briefly here because of the important role they and their commercial system played in the affairs of southern Africa. They were the product of centuries of intermarriage between Arab colonists and Bantu-speaking settlers along more than a thousand miles of Indian Ocean coast.

Their homeland was the coastal belt, and the numerous islands just offshore, that stretched from Somalia to Mozambique. By the time of ,Mutota the Swahili had built more than a score of thriving cities in Somalia, Kenya, and Tanzania, and their commercial agents moved industriously up the river valleys leading inland from the Mozambique coast. Kilwa, on the coast of southern Tanzania, was their southernmost city, but they had established sizable commercial stations in Mozambique and had long been active in Karanga affairs. They had no political or territorial ambitions in the strong Rozwi-Karanga kingdom, but it was decidedly in their commercial interest for the Rozwi to expand their control over the vast gold- and copper-mining areas of the Rhodesian plateau.

Mutota assembled a large army and campaigned almost ceaselessly for at least ten years, until about 1450. By that time he had seized firm control over most of modern Rhodesia, between the Zambezi and the Limpopo, although he was less successful in the far west and the mountainous east.

114

As soon as he subdued an area, Mutota installed a Rozwi lieutenant as governor and exacted promises of annual tribute and contingents of soldiers from the chiefs and kings in the territory who were now his vassals. The tribute had to be paid in grain, gold dust, ivory, salt, cattle, and copper. Each vassal was further required to supply men to help build and maintain roads, to fight in Mutota's army, and to serve as bearers and canoemen for transporting trade goods to Sofala and the coast.

The success of Mutota's campaigns brought an increase in the flow of wealth and trade goods into his court, although a portion was retained by his Rozwi governors to enrich themselves and finance the expenses of their courts and troops. Some of the gold, copper, and ivory was used to fashion lavish ornaments for the Rozwi nobility and their wives, while the rest was used to trade with the Swahili for cloth, iron tools and weapons, beads, china, and glass vessels. The tribute of salt, grain, and cattle was used to support the large retinues of the king, his army, and his vassals.

Although it is not known for sure whether Mutota's expansion marked the first Rozwi occupation of Zimbabwe, the archeological record shows that a new period of construction began there in about

115

1440–1450. For four centuries after that time Zimbabwe was under the control of the Rozwi, and its greatest achievements in building occurred under them. Their stonemasons completed the work that had been done on the Acropolis, greatly refining it and adding many beautiful archways, steps, platforms for art and statuary, and small enclosures for worship. They built the Great Enclosure in the valley, perfecting the techniques of stonework which resulted in the extremely smooth and regular upper walls, the Conical Tower, and the chevron patterns.

From later historical records we know that the Rozwi used the basic Karanga religious system to solidify their rule. They preached that Mwari's blessings could be obtained most effectively through the great Rozwi ancestors in the spirit world, and that only Rozwi rulers and priests could communicate properly with these ancestors. By this period of Rozwi rule the Rhodesian plateau had become heavily populated, so that a period of drought or an invasion of locusts could bring widespread famine and suffering. The people's dependence on their Rozwi rulers thus became even greater, for it was felt that only the spiritual power of the Rozwi royalty was strong enough to appeal to Mwari for desperately needed rain and relief from natural disasters. The Rozwi devoted much attention, therefore, to expanding and beautifying Zimbabwe and the other great religious-political centers of Karangaland.

Mutota, the great founding king of the Rozwi empire, died in 1450 with his imperial dream only partially a reality. His successes were great, however, and he was given a name of awe and respect by the peoples he conquered, which after his death became the name of his empire: Mwene Mutapa. In Shona, *Mwene Mutapa* means "master pillager," and both his own people and those he conquered recognized in Mutota a master of conquest and spoils.

Mwene Mutapa (from a seventeenth-century French portrait)

Mutope, Mutota's son, succeeded his father and continued the imperial campaign with great success for the next thirty years until his death in 1480. He brought the eastern lands under his control, so that the empire of Mwene Mutapa stretched to the Indian Ocean. At the time of his death the empire was one of the largest ever created in Africa south of the equator, and rivaled the great West African empires of Ghana, Mali, and Songhai in extent.

The sheer size of Mwene Mutapa, however, brought serious problems of government. Mutota and Mutope were able to insure the loyalty of their Rozwi vassals by the force of their personalities and the great strength of the army of conquest they had assembled and maintained for forty years. But in-

117

side the empire communications were difficult over such vast distances; there were many centers of local pride and cultural diversity; and the Rozwi vassals were not a tame, obedient class of administrators.

The great empire was shattered almost immediately after Mutope's death, when its southern half broke free. Mutope had installed a powerful Rozwi noble named Changa as governor of the southern lands, and Changa ruled the earlier kingdom of Butua from the capital at Zimbabwe. Swahili and Arab traders soon entered his province eagerly, for it included the numerous gold mines upon which much of Mwene Mutapa's wealth depended. Either in flattery or from sincere respect these foreigners began to refer to Changa as "Changa Amir," which in Arabic implied that Changa was the supreme ruler of his province. Changa developed a direct trade link with the Swahili, so that rich goods flowed directly into his capital. Although he continued loyally to pay the required tribute to Mutope, it was clear that his power was rapidly increasing.

When Mutope died in 1480, and his son Nyahuma became *Mwene Mutapa*, Changa decided that the time had come to establish his autonomy. He officially changed his name and that of his country to Changamire, adopting the Swahili title of praise, and refused to pay further tribute to the *Mwene Mutapa*. War followed. Changamire successfully defeated Nyahuma and seized control of the entire empire, which he ruled from 1490 to 1494. Then Nyahuma's son raised an army in the northern territory, marched against Changamire,

118

and killed him in battle without completely destroying his army. The result was that the *Mwene Mutapa* line regained control of the northern portion of the empire, while Changamire's son, Changamire II, was able to retain control over the southern portion, including both his father's original lands and the eastern and southeastern parts of the *Mwene Mutapa's* lands. Both kingdoms were still extensive, and both had direct access to the Indian Ocean, but neither possessed the power to rule the other.

When the first Portuguese ships arrived on the Mozambique coast and installed a mission at Sofala in 1505, they soon learned that there were two powerful kingdoms in the interior, from both of which flowed considerable quantities of gold, ivory, and other prized goods. And the arrival of the Portuguese ushers in a new phase in the history of southern Africa.

At the time of Portuguese contact the nations of Mwene Mutapa (which the Portuguese corrupted to Monomotapa) and Changamire were roughly equal in strength and territory. But Mwene Mutapa, bordering on the great Zambezi, still functioned as the more important trade channel, because ivory, metals, and slaves were brought down the Zambezi from a vast inland area that included parts of Zambia, Malawi, Tanzania, and Zaire. Changamire contained more mineral deposits, but the interior market it drew on was not as extensive as that of Mwene Mutapa. The Portuguese therefore concentrated their attention on the Zambezi and Mwene Mutapa, and sent explorers to the kingdom as early as 1514.

The history of the Rhodesian plateau before the arrival of the Portuguese is known only through archeology and oral history, although the evidence from both sources agrees on the basic facts. Further, the names and exploits of kings passed from generation to generation by history tellers has been verified quite accurately, at least back to Mutota, by comparing them with the written evidence left in Portuguese records from the early sixteenth century on. After the arrival of the Portuguese written records exist, so that the history of Mwene Mutapa is almost as well known as that of Kongo during the same period.

The Portuguese influence proved as disastrous for Mwene Mutapa as it did for Kongo. By about 1550 Portuguese treatie: had been negotiated with Mwene Mutapa to regulate trade, and Portuguese outposts had been established at Sena and Tete in the Zambezi valley. For many years, however, the

120

Portuguese made little effort to interfere in the internal affairs of Mwene Mutapa, because their major problem was the elimination of the Arab and Swahili traders who had for so long dominated the trade with the interior.

The Portuguese had both religious and economic reasons to force a speedy demise of the Swahili commercial system. The Swahili and Arab traders were experts, skilled in their relationships with the peoples of the inland kingdoms. And they were Muslims, spiritually and intellectually allied with the great Islamic civilization of North Africa and the Mediterranean that the aggressively Christian Portuguese regarded as their archenemy. Within a few decades the Portuguese had brutally destroyed many of the beautiful and civilized Swahili coastal cities, and had began to intrigue against the Swahili presence in Mwene Mutapa. By 1600 Swahili influence in Mwene Mutapa was steadily declining, while that of the Portuguese was growing. By about 1650 the Portuguese were supreme, and the *Mwene Mutapa* depended upon Portuguese support to maintain his kingdom's prosperity and security.

Changamire remained largely immune to the slow subversive spread of Portuguese power. It was less accessible to Portuguese contact, and maintained a coolness toward the Portuguese because they were allies of the *Mwene Mutapa*. Yet the Changamire kings were fully aware of the extent of Portuguese influence in Mwene Mutapa, and they regarded it as a danger to their own security.

In 1693 the *Mwene Mutapa* appealed to the reigning *Changamire*, Dombo, to drive the Portuguese from his kingdom, and Dombo was only too eager to oblige. In a ruthless war of two years' duration, Dombo killed or drove out all the Portuguese in the southern and western portions of Mwene Mutapa, stopping only when he reached the Portuguese bastion at Tete. Although he did not attempt to take Tete and Sena, he effectively cleansed most of Mwene Mutapa of the Portuguese presence. Unfortunately for the *Mwene Mutapa*, Dombo decided to incorporate much of the conquered territory into the empire of Changamire, and neither the *Mwene Mutapa* nor the Portuguese were able to prevent him. Later *Mwene Mutapa*s were reduced to rulership of a shrunken territory that could be administered with Portuguese support in the region of Tete and Sena, while Changamire prospered as a great empire too strong for the Portuguese to attack. For the next fifty years the Portuguese activities inland from Tete depended almost entirely on the good will of the *Changamires*; not until the 1880's did Portugal gain political and military control over the inland areas of Mozambique.

The Portuguese conquest of the coasts of eastern Africa reduced the volume of trade for many years, but Changamire proved to be surprisingly strong without it. Between 1600 and 1800 Changamire flourished, despite little contact with the outside world. This was the period of greatest achievement at Zimbabwe and other stone-building centers, and the magnificence of the Rozwi construction during the period still shows itself in the ruins. Apart from its acquisition of part of Mwene Mutapa, Changamire did not expand much

122

during the period, and its rulers seemed content to concentrate on internal affairs, especially the strengthening of the great centers of wealth, religion, and political power that Zimbabwe symbolizes.

The period 1600–1800 marks the flowering of the Bantu civilization in Rhodesia. Although there seems to have been relatively little change in the way of life of the ordinary people, and little change in their techniques of agriculture, the material culture under Rozwi influence evolved to a new high. The techniques of stonemasonry reached their highest development, and are impressive when compared to the stonework of any ancient civilization in the world. Pottery making was greatly refined. Beautiful pots and bowls with thin walls and smoothly polished sides were made in large numbers. Many of the pots were decorated with finely drawn symbols and bands and designs of several colors. Small figurines of both animals and human beings were fashioned from clay, showing considerable artistic sensitivity.

In the homes and courts of the Rozwi rulers wealth abounded. Plaques and ornaments sheathed in gold were common, as were numerous chests of beads, bracelets, bangles, belts, and other objects made from shells and gold. Even utilitarian articles such as combs were beautifully made, sometimes of gold. Karanga artisans made fine points for swords, arrows, and spears, as well as scissors, hoes, axes, and other tools and weapons of iron, although some of these objects were imported from India and Arabia. Houses were built of stone and *daga,* and those of the nobility were quite large.

123

By 1800, however, storm clouds were beginning to gather. Within a few decades the great Changamire empire would fall apart, and with it much of the peace and prosperity of all Shonaland.

Inside Shonaland population had steadily increased, but by the end of the eighteenth century there were few underpopulated lands in southern Africa into which its peoples could migrate. The fertility of much of the Rhodesian plateau is limited. As population increased, the land began to reach its maximum ability to support the people, and families found it difficult to produce more than enough food for simple subsistence.

More serious was a similar condition far to the south, in the Natal and Transvaal provinces of South Africa, where European settlers had been expanding toward the north since the seventeenth century. By the 1790's land pressure in the territories of the Zulu and Swazi peoples was intense, and a powerful military state was created by the Zulu. As this state expanded it created major upheavals of both its own and surrounding peoples. The result was a series of migrations by large groups of trained warriors, several of which moved toward the north, into Mozambique and the Rhodesian plateau.

Three detachments of these conquering bands participated in a series of invasions which destroyed Changamire between 1830 and 1860.

One was led by Soshangane, a chief of a clan closely related to the Zulu, who abandoned his lands in the face of overwhelming pressure from the main Zulu army and migrated to the north through Swaziland into southern Mozambique. Af-

124

ter entering Mozambique, Soshangane's forces marshaled their strength and began to subdue the chiefdoms and villages that lay in their path. From a center of strength in southern Mozambique they expanded their new kingdom northward and westward into Changamire, incorporating much of eastern Changamire into a new empire which was called Gaza. Between 1820 and 1830 Soshangane's troops crushed all opposition in their new territory and forced the Portuguese trading settlements to acknowledge their supremacy. With their successes, the few remnants of Mwene Mutapa's power disappeared.

The second invasion was led by Zwangendaba, who brought another force of defeated Zulu warriors northward in the same path. Encountering Soshangane's army in southern Mozambique, Zwangendaba was soundly defeated, and his army fled toward the northwest, straight into the heartland of Changamire, which it entered in 1831. Although it suffered reverses for a time, it soon began to grow stronger by absorbing conquered soldiers. By 1833 Zwangendaba was master of a formidable troop, and he continued to march into central Changamire. In 1834 his troops entered Zimbabwe, quickly defeated its feeble defenses, and sacked the great center. They seized many of the objects of gold and copper, and attempted to demolish a number of the stone buildings and walls. After a few months of pillaging they moved north again, crossing the Zambezi in 1835 and continuing their migration northward until they eventually settled in Malawi and Tanzania.

By 1835 Changamire was prostrate. Its capital

125

and greatest national shrine had been desecrated, its eastern lands had been conquered, and the power of its Rozwi nobility had virtually disappeared. But a third blow fell in the 1840's, when a third contingent of invaders from Zululand, the Matabele under the leadership of Mzilikazi, invaded Changamire's western territories and settled there permanently. Mzilikazi's band had wandered for nearly twenty years through the Transvaal, where it was frequently harassed by other African forces and by Boer militiamen from the expanding European settlements in the Transvaal. It acquired the name Matabele (or Ndebele) from the phrase "those who disappear out of sight behind their immense Zulu war shields of stout cowhide," and Mzilikazi's people have continued to use the name proudly. Today they occupy the western portion of Rhodesia, now called Matabeleland to distinguish it from Mashonaland, where the Shona peoples of the once great Changamire empire live.

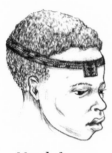

Matabele man

By 1850 the Changamire empire was only a memory. Local Rozwi chiefs continued to live around Zimbabwe for some years, but by 1885 the site was abandoned completely. The devastation of both the shrine and the empire was so complete that most living Shona peoples cannot give details of their illustrious past. They remember that once their land was a proud and powerful kingdom, and their legends tell of the struggles of Mutota, Mutope, Changamire, and their successors. But the legends become entangled with destruction after 1800; only the ancient respect for the Rozwi has survived, and even that has deteriorated under nearly a century of European occupation and rule.

126

Thus ended another notable chapter in the story of the growth of the Bantu civilization. Struggling against unknown lands and strange environments, the ancient Bantu-speaking ancestors penetrated the Rhodesian plateau and southern Africa as they did in so many other areas, and there they built a great empire with noble monuments in stone to attest their former glory. But a sad combination of natural forces, uncertain rains, infertile soil, and the aggressive encroachments of both Africans and Europeans eventually brought both Mwene Mutapa and Changamire to their death. Only the undeniable evidence of their achievements in stone building and the patient research of archeologists and historians reveal the heights to which they rose.

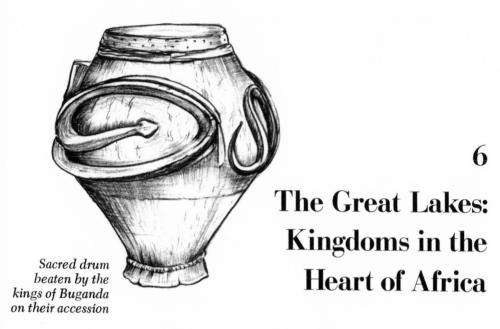

Sacred drum beaten by the kings of Buganda on their accession

6

The Great Lakes: Kingdoms in the Heart of Africa

At the same time that families of the early Bantu-speaking farmers were expanding southward from Katanga onto the plateaus of Zambia and Rhodesia, other groups were pressing northward. Soon they reached the region of the Great Lakes of East Africa, and by about A.D. 500 began to settle most of the lands around those lakes. Here they slowed their expansion, for the lands were rich and the territory farther north was being occupied by other African peoples.

In the country around the Great Lakes, which scholars often call the Interlacustrine Region (or region between the lakes), the ancestors of the Bantu farmers sank their roots and quickly began to build another center of the Bantu civilization.

Although this new country was long isolated from developments both in other parts of Africa and in the outside world, its great fertility allowed the new immigrants to build one of the most impressive and illustrious centers of their far-flung civilization.

The Interlacustrine Region is not large, as African territories go. It stretches an average of about 300 miles between Lakes Tanganyika, Kivu, Edward, and Albert on the east and Lake Victoria Nyanza on the west, and it extends perhaps 800 miles north and south from Lake Kioga to Lake Tanganyika. But it is high country, with elevations of 3,500 to more than 6,000 feet above sea level, which makes it cool despite being near the equator. Its high altitudes and numerous mountains attract moisture-bearing clouds from the Indian Ocean and the lakes, which bring the area a high rainfall. Much of its soil was formed by ancient volcanic activity, so that it is deep and fertile.

Geography influences the development of civilization and the course of history in every part of the world, and its role in the building of the Interlacustrine Bantu civilization is especially important. The area of this civilization lies along a series of massive highlands that stretch through the interior of eastern Africa, from Ethiopia to South Africa, like a giant spine. Volcanic mountains are dotted throughout this high continental mass, and they include the highest and most spectacular peaks in Africa: Mount Kilimanjaro, the highest peak; Mount Kenya; Mount Meru; Mount Elgon; and the towering peaks of the Ruwenzori Mountains. All of these peaks are snow-capped for most of the year.

129

More than a million years ago, in eastern Africa, a subterranean upheaval caused the surface of the earth to fold over itself. This in turn created an extensive crack, which originates in the Sea of Galilee and the Jordan River Valley; then runs southward through the Red Sea, the highlands of Ethiopia, and down through East Africa; and then finally turns eastward and ends in the Indian Ocean between Mozambique and Madagascar. In Ethiopia this rift splits, one branch continuing southward through Kenya and Tanzania to Lake Malawi. The other branch runs southwest, through Uganda and Tanzania, where it forms the border country between these states and Zaire; then it bends southeast to rejoin the main rift in Lake Malawi.

In the main rift, called the Great Rift, lie numerous shallow lakes. In East Africa these lakes include Rudolph, Nakuru, Naivasha, Natron, Manyara, Eyasi, and Rukwa. Most are less than 300 feet in maximum depth and their waters are highly alkaline, since they have no outlets. Water flows into them from the surrounding higher country, then remains except for evaporation. The Great Rift runs through spectacularly high country in Kenya, sometimes over 9,000 feet above sea level. There the rift is well marked, its sides more than 2,000 feet high. One can stand on one edge and look thirty to fifty miles across the rift in this area, seeing the huge valley spread below like a giant channel cut through the land.

The other rift, called the Western Rift, is somewhat less spectacular in the views it affords, but in one way it is even more dramatic. Its valley contains a series of long, narrow lakes, the chief ones

THE INTERLACUSTRINE REGION AND KINGDOMS c. 1700

(SUDAN)   (ETHIOPIA)

                           Lake Rudolf
        (UGANDA)
KITARA   BUNYORO
Lake Albert
                Lake Kyoga
                BUGANDA
ANKOLE
Lake Edward

INTERLACUSTRINE REGION

                    Lake Victoria Nyanza
Lake Kivu   (KENYA)
RWANDA
BURUNDI   KARAGWE

Lake Tanganyika

(ZAIRE)   (TANZANIA)

                Lake Rukwa
Lake Mweru

            (ZAMBIA)   Lake Nyasa

            (MALAWI)
                    (MOZAMBIQUE)

                Zambesi River

    (RHODESIA)   Louise E. Jefferson

being Tanganyika, Kivu, Edward, and Albert, which are extremely deep. Lake Tanganyika, whose maximum depth is 4,708 feet, is the second deepest lake in the world, after the Soviet Union's Lake Baikal. The lakes of the Western Rift are, in several cases, connected with each other, and all have outlets that allow their waters to flow into rivers. From these rivers the great Nile originates, as does the Congo, so that the Great Lakes of the Western Rift are the source of the two mightiest rivers on the African continent.

Between the two rifts, in a massive shallow basin that lies more than 3,500 feet above sea level, is Lake Victoria Nyanza, the second largest lake in the world, almost equaling Lake Superior in area. It is the country to Victoria Nyanza's north, west, and south that forms the Interlacustrine Region, stretching from this immense lake to the lakes of the Western Rift.

The Interlacustrine Region is isolated from the rest of the continent. On the north lie the vast swamps and marshes bordering the upper Nile, which even today are difficult to cross. On the west, in Zaire, lies the great tropical rain forest of the Congo Basin. On the east there is an arid belt that separates the lake area from the Indian Ocean coast, and this belt is as wide as 600 miles in many places. It has always been sparsely inhabited, and has been an uninviting land for travelers as well as for farmers.

Only to the south is there clear, settled country between the Interlacustrine area and other centers of population and civilization, and there lie the great Bantu states of the Luba, Lunda, Bemba, and their relatives east of Lake Tanganyika. It was from this country that the Bantu-speaking farmers moved into the Interlacustrine Region. Whether there were close contacts between the two regions during the millennium after the migrations is not known. Similarities in language and pottery from archeological sites show the common origins of the peoples who lived there, but neither archeology nor any historical evidence reveals any continuing contact and influence later on.

Today the Interlacustrine Region contains the states of Burundi, Rwanda, most of Uganda, and eastern Tanzania. Zaire's western borders touch it, and the affairs of eastern Kenya are influenced by its peoples. The colonial conquest at the end of the nineteenth century created these modern states, but three—Burundi, Rwanda, and Uganda— grew directly out of the ancient kingdoms which dominated the history of the region for many centuries.

The first Bantu farmers arrived in the Interlacustrine Region as early as A.D. 500 or 600, but they were not the first immigrants. The area was inhabited long before their arrival by other, very different peoples, and is in fact adjacent to the country in which mankind probably first appeared. The plains between the Great Rift and the lakes, today rather dry and uninviting but densely populated by vast herds of wild animals, have yielded the most important evidence of human evolution in the world. At such famous sites as Olduvai Gorge, Olorgesailie, and the Lake Rudolph–Omo River area, in Tanzania, in Kenya, and in southern Ethiopia, anthropologists have found abundant remains of creatures that range from ancestral primates, living 40 million years ago, right up to modern man. From these sites have come the numerous remains of *Australopithecus, Homo erectus,* and other ancient ancestors of humanity.

In the millennia before the first Bantu farmers arrived, three groups were living in the Interlacustrine Region and in the lands adjacent to it. One group was ancestral to today's Pygmies, small bands of whom still live in Uganda, Rwanda, and eastern Zaire. Making their living by hunting wild animals in the forested parts of the region, and by gathering wild fruits, seeds, vegetables, and insects, the Pygmies were ultimately affected so deeply by the incoming Bantu that they have long spoken only Bantu languages, and their own languages are extinct.

Pygmy man

The second group was the Khoisan, who hunted and gathered wild foods in the drier plains. Their territory once stretched all the way from the southern tip of Africa to the Ethiopian highlands. In East Africa they were completely absorbed by the Bantu immigrants, although there are several small ethnic groups in Tanzania who speak languages that are thought to be of the Khoisan stock. These people, such as the Hadzapi, are racially similar to their Bantu neighbors today, but they still live mainly by hunting and cling to their own language.

The third group was the Cushites, a tall, brown-skinned people who were related to the peoples of Ethiopia and Somalia; their modern representatives include the Galla of Ethiopia and Somalia, the Somali, and the Sidamo of Ethiopia. There is ar-

134

cheological evidence that these Cushites sent small parties southward into Tanzania and Kenya as early as 10,000 B.C., during the Stone Age. They seem to have lived mainly in the region of the Great Rift Valley and along the coast. Whether they ever settled farther east, in the Interlacustrine Region itself, is not clear. Like the early Pygmies and Khoisans, however, they were absorbed by the Bantu, leaving only traces of their existence in the modern peoples of the area. A few small groups, such as the Iraqw (whom the Bantu call Mbuli) of Tanzania, still speak Cushitic languages, although they cannot be distinguished racially from their Bantu neighbors.

The Cushites are believed to have begun the practice of agriculture in East Africa even before the arrival of the Bantu. They had learned, from their more advanced relatives in Ethiopia, how to build terraces of stone on steep hillsides and how to dig channels through which water could be diverted from streams to irrigate the terraces. The Bantu farmers are thought to have learned these techniques from the ancient Cushites, although in most of the Interlacustrine Region the soil is sufficiently level, fertile, and well watered to make terracing or irrigation unnecessary. Some of the Bantu farmers of East Africa who have settled in areas where terracing and irrigation are desirable use this technique, but most use the shifting-plot method.

The study of East Africa's prehistory and history has established the fact that the Pygmies, Khoisans, and Cushites lived in parts of the country, rather thinly populated, before the Bantu farmers

Cushite soldier

135

came. But whether any of them had an appreciable influence on the Bantu settlers is much less clear. By and large they seem to have been absorbed or exterminated—probably the former—leaving only minor remnants and traces to mark their long settlement in the region. The early history of East Africa, and especially of the Interlacustrine Region, is therefore almost entirely a history of the Bantu immigrants: their expansion over the area, their clearing of the lands, and their creation of a dense population which eventually formed a chain of small states and kingdoms. The later history of the area is the story of how these small states and kingdoms developed into larger ones, several becoming empires and powerful, long-lived nations that influenced events far beyond their own borders.

When the first ancestors of the Bantu farmers came, they found a natural environment richer than any forebears had ever settled. The cool altitudes, fertile soils, high rainfall, and numerous lakes and rivers were ideal for farming. The early farmers planted many crops of millet, sorghum, and beans, peas, and other vegetables, all of which grew well everywhere except in the wettest areas. At some time during the first few centuries of Bantu settlement a new group of crops came into widespread use, and these were even better adapted to the region than the traditional ones.

The new crops originated in Asia, mainly in Indonesia, and included Asian yams, bananas, plantains, and coco yams. These plants were developed in moist, tropical rain forests, and they spread quickly into the moist forests of central

136

and western Africa. How they reached Africa is not known for certain, although they are believed to have been brought by about A.D. 100, if not earlier, by mariners from either India or Indonesia. There is little evidence of Indonesians visiting the African mainland, but they settled the great island of Madagascar off the Mozambique coast. Today that island's national language, Malagasy, is an Indo-Polynesian language, and the majority of its peoples are descended from the early Indonesian settlers.

The valuable plants that these ancient Indonesians used in their Asian homeland may have reached Africa by way of Madagascar, although it is equally possible that they were brought directly to the African mainland by mariners who sailed around the perimeter of the Indian Ocean, touching in Persia, Arabia, and Somalia on their voyages south. However, when the plants arrived they spread, during the first millennium of the Christian era, into the Interlacustrine Region as well as into the vast rain forests of the Congo Basin, then into the rain forests of West Africa. By about A.D. 1000 Africans in all these areas were cultivating them, along with the indigenous plants they had grown earlier.

Bananas and plantains were admirably suited to the moist lands around Lake Victoria Nyanza, and provided a highly nutritious source of food that could be grown and harvested with little effort. When the early Bantu farmers added them to the millet and sorghum they were already growing, they had the means to support a large population in a relatively small area. Between about A.D. 500

137

and 1000 their population is believed to have expanded very rapidly, until finally they were more densely settled than any other African people outside the Nile Valley.

As their populations expanded, the Bantu farmers began to develop governments to maintain internal tranquillity, to settle disputes over land ownership and rights, and to protect themselves against encroachment from neighboring groups. As early as A.D. 1000 small states began to develop in parts of the Interlacustrine Region, and by about 1200 there were numerous small kingdoms.

The growth of the Interlacustrine kingdoms during this early period is still a little-known part of the area's history. Archeologists have not yet explored enough sites to give a very clear picture, and the region was so isolated from the outside world that there are no written records before the nineteenth century. Even for later periods the history of the area is best known through an analysis of the oral traditions that each kingdom has passed down from generation to generation, and oral traditions seldom reveal more than a hazy picture of developments in very ancient times.

The oral traditions of the Interlacustrine peoples are, however, surprisingly rich sources of information. There are more than a hundred groups in the region which have elaborate traditions covering a long period of time. For several of the older kingdoms, such as Buganda, the traditions cover twenty or more generations. Since a generation spans approximately thirty years, this gives information for six centuries. Oral traditions list the names of kings, together with their major adventures and achieve-

138

Baganda king

ments. Frequently they give the names of the kings'
wives, their notable brothers and sons, and their
most important enemies and allies. They rarely tell
with any precision how long the kings reigned, but
astronomy steps in at this point to add more information: oral traditions often mention eclipses
of the sun or moon, to which this science can give
precise dates.

When historians piece together the numerous
oral histories that have been recorded, and add
dates from astronomy and archeology, an outline
of Interlacustrine history begins to emerge.

The earliest dates for which the names of kings
are known come in the period 1300–1400, but it is
apparent that states of some kind were already in
existence when these ancient kings came to power.
Most of the Interlacustrine kingdoms begin their
histories with the rule of a dynasty of kings known
as the Chwezi; the names and identities of rulers
before the Chwezi have not been included in the

139

traditions. The Chwezi are credited with the founding of many of the kingdoms, and tradition has endowed them with great nobility and power. Often they are described as godlike. They were members of a widely spread royal clan; the name Chwezi is a clan name. Individual members of the clan became rulers, and their family ties helped to unite many of the Interlacustrine kingdoms into a loose confederation as early as 1300. This confederation included such eventually famous states as Buganda, Bunyoro, Karagwe, Burundi, and Rwanda, together with dozens of lesser known states.

How these kingdoms developed during and after their Chwezi reigns is best seen through the history of the two great kingdoms of Uganda, Bunyoro and Buganda. Both are very old, and both have retained their identities as proud kingdoms up to today.

Of the two, Bunyoro was by far the greater in ancient times. Under Chwezi rule it was known as Kitara, and it seems to have been virtually an empire during the fourteenth century. At that time Buganda was a tiny state, no more than about fifty miles across, located on the shores of Lake Victoria Nyanza near the site of the modern city of Kampala. It had a relationship to Kitara as a vassal state whose Chwezi king owed fealty to the great Chwezi king of Kitara.

The legends of Bunyoro tell of other dynasties that ruled Kitara even before the Chwezi: the Gabu and the Ranzi. Little detail is given for these ancient dynasties, however, except that they were revered as having had divine qualities and were

Banyoro drummer   140

placed in power by God after He had created mankind. They possessed vast herds of cattle, as almost all Interlacustrine nobility have since time immemorial, and had special symbols of rulership that were handed on to their successors: copper gongs, rods of copper and iron, shell ornaments, and sacred drums.

Burundi drummer

One of the great mysteries of ancient Interlacustrine history is the identity of the Chwezi and their mythical predecessors. Were they Bantu kings, or were they conquerors from elsewhere who moved into Uganda and seized power over the Bantu farmers? There are hints that they were not Bantu. The Bantu farmers of the Interlacustrine area have never devoted much time to herding cattle but have instead cultivated the soil. The names of the ancient Gabu and Ranzi dynasties are the names of clans that still exist farther to the south, among the Watutsi rulers of the kingdom of Rwanda and among the seminomadic Bahima peoples who herd cattle in many parts of southern Uganda. Both the Watutsi and the Bahima are racially different from the surrounding Bantu, being much taller and sharper in facial features, even though they speak Bantu languages.

A few authorities have speculated that the ancient Chwezi and their mythical predecessors may have been Cushites, who were absorbed by the Bantu but eventually seized power and set themselves up as a ruling class. Others believe that they were Bantu who adopted the practice of herding cattle from pastoral peoples to the north, then acquired power because of their military prowess and bravery. Still others believe that they were immi-

141

grants from the north who filtered into the country as early as 1100 or 1200 and conquered the peaceful Bantu farmers. There is too little concrete evidence available to prove or disprove any of these hypotheses, although it is quite clear that the Chwezi and other ruling dynasties of most Interlacustrine states were different in many respects from the mass of people over whom they ruled. If they were not immigrants they were assuredly influenced by cattle-herding peoples to the north who are very different from the Bantu.

The land of Bunyoro is the northernmost outpost of the Bantu-speaking peoples of the Interlacustrine Region. On its west it is bounded by the Ruwenzori Mountains, whose high, jagged peaks are snow-capped the year round. On its east it is bounded by the Nile, although Bunyoro power has long been felt east of that river. The country is neither as fertile nor as moist as the lands around Lake Victoria Nyanza, but it is good for both grain farming and cattle. Its high plains are covered with grasses that provide excellent pastures.

This grassy country stretches far to the north, deep into the republic of Sudan. There, around the Nile and its major tributaries, vast swamps cover much of the land during the rainy season, and the land is excellent for cattle but poor for farming. In this northern country live the Nilotic peoples, who speak languages of the large Sudanic language stock that covers much of north-central Africa. The Nilotic peoples tend to be very tall, their men averaging over six feet in some groups, and they are slender.

Political upheavals in northeastern Africa were

Uganda warrior

142

common throughout ancient and medieval history, due to the rise and decline of various Nubian and Ethiopian civilizations and the gradual invasion of the country by Arabs between A.D. 700 and 1600. These upheavals, accompanied by a continuing increase in population, resulted in a steady push of the Nilotic peoples toward the south. They have long been present in the northernmost part of Uganda, and in the past few centuries have pushed deep into East Africa, as far south as northern Tanzania. Because of their southward movements, they have inevitably influenced the course of history in the Bantu lands of the Interlacustrine Region, even though that area has been too densely populated by Bantu farmers to permit extensive settlement by the Nilotes.

The history of the Interlacustrine Region after the sixteenth century was heavily influenced by invasions of Nilotes. It is quite possible, therefore, that they had penetrated the region long before that time, and either founded or influenced the Chwezi and related dynasties.

Kitara, under the Chwezi dynasty, covered a much larger territory than later Bunyoro did. The kingdoms of Toro and Ankole seem to have been included in its lands, as were Buganda and a number of other small kingdoms. Then, during the fourteenth and fifteenth centuries, a series of Nilotic invasions occurred. By about 1500 Kitara had been conquered by the invaders, and a new phase of Interlacustrine history began.

The Nilotic invaders came in large family groups of several hundred people each. These groups maintained contact with each other so that they

143

could join together for military purposes when necessary. After settling the lands of northern Uganda, they began to seize parts of Kitara and to subject its Bantu farmers to their rule. The leading clan of Nilotes was the Bito, and their leaders soon became the nobility of northern Kitara. As they intermarried with the local people, they came to be called the Banyoro, and their kingdom Bunyoro. From Bunyoro their well-organized raiding parties fanned out to the south and east, gradually forcing the Chwezi aristocracy from power in other kingdoms and replacing them with Bito.

According to legend the Bito were related to the Chwezi, and were welcomed by them. Many traditions in Bunyoro tell how the Chwezi sent messengers to the north to summon their Bito cousins to take over the reins of government. When the Bito arrived, so traditions say, they were given the royal symbols of office by the Chwezi and invested with power, following which the Chwezi departed into obscurity. Even the wives of the Chwezi were given over to the Bito, according to tradition.

These accounts are classic examples of how history can be falsified to suit the convenience of those who have control of the records—in this case oral accounts. The Chwezi did not summon the Bito or welcome their arrival; they resisted. In western and southern Uganda there are numerous ruins of towns which were surrounded by large earthen embankments erected to ward off attack by warriors and to provide shelter for the king, his many wives and children, his large retinue, and his vast herds of cattle. The largest of these towns, Bigo, is more than two miles in diameter, and the con-

144

struction of its massive earth walls took years of arduous labor by thousands of workers. Archeologists estimate that Bigo was occupied about 1350, then was abandoned. It was almost certainly a Chwezi capital in the south of Kitara, where the king defended himself against the frequent attacks of the Bito-led Nilotic invaders.

The Bito were culturally less developed than the refined Bantu whose lands they invaded, and they found it necessary to make their rule seem as legitimate as possible in order to prevent popular opposition and rebellion. This they did by intermarrying with the Chwezi aristocracy and by altering the oral accounts of their arrival to make them seem less like alien conquerors and more like relatives who had been welcomed by a tired Chwezi dynasty. After a few generations they succeeded. Their descendants were still known as Bito, and claimed a divine right to rule. But they were related to local families by intermarriage, spoke the local language, and observed important local customs. Like the Chwezi, they disdained farming and prided themselves on maintaining large herds of cattle. Their wealth and prestige were reflected in the size of their herds.

Under Bito rule Bunyoro set about the task of trying to rebuild the old Chwezi empire of Kitara. Within a century or two Bito aristocracy was established in most of the kingdoms of northern and central Uganda, and Bunyoro's armies were raiding as far south as Rwanda. As Bito power expanded it created a confederation of loosely knit kingdoms, in which each chief or king was acknowledged as the hereditary ruler of his state but also paid

145

nominal tribute to the *Mukama,* as the king of Bunyoro was known.

Within Bunyoro itself the *Mukama* ruled through an elaborate government of appointed chiefs and district administrators, most of whom were Bito. He had numerous wives; the last independent *Mukama,* Kabarega, who ruled late in the nineteenth century, left 140 children. Around him were scores of ministers, most of whom were also administrators of local districts, spending a part of the year at the capital. There were important title holders who were in charge of the bodyguard, the royal symbols of office, the royal household, the collection of tribute, and the education of the *Mukama's* sons. The capital moved from time to time, but it consisted of hundreds of large houses made of wooden frameworks covered with plaited grass and reeds, often in beautiful designs. Stone, which is rare in most of the Interlacustrine area, was never used as a building material.

During the sixteenth and seventeenth centuries Bunyoro was at the peak of its development, and its influence was felt throughout the northern half of the Interlacustrine Region. To its south, in such kingdoms as Ankole, Karagwe, Rwanda, and Burundi, which were not under Bito rule, the local Bahima and Watutsi ruling aristocracy had developed stronger governments and armies in order to resist attacks from Bunyoro.

At this time Buganda was only one of many small states within the sphere of Bunyoro influence. According to Buganda tradition that kingdom had been founded by a great culture hero named Kintu ("the marvel"), who had come into the country

146

from the northeast and had organized the kingdom by performing wondrous feats of magic and personal prowess. Kintu's legendary reign was so long that most historians believe he was not a person but a symbol of an early dynastic period, dated prior to 1300. Legend holds that he eventually united the heads of the numerous Baganda clans, which number more than a hundred, so that all their chiefs accepted him as *Kabaka* ("king"). He then moved on, to some place unknown to mortals, and was succeeded by an equally marvelous king named Chwa ("Chwezi"), who kept the kingdom united and established many of its cherished customs.

Then, according to tradition, Chwa moved on and was succeeded quite peacefully by Kimera, the first of a Bito dynasty. The traditions of Bunyoro claim that Buganda was given to Kimera by his relative Mukama Rukidi, who ruled Bunyoro seventeen generations back, or around 1400–1450. This date is probably roughly correct, since eclipses reported as having occurred in later generations corroborate it.

After Kimera became *Kabaka* of Buganda he followed the practices adopted by other Bito nobles when they seized power in Interlacustrine states. He took a number of Baganda women from prominent clans as wives. He used all the royal emblems, robes, and regalia of his Chwezi predecessor, and asserted that he ruled with the same authority as the Chwezi.

Buganda, however, was a rather different kingdom from Bunyoro and most others in the region. Although it was small in area, it had a large, homo-

147

geneous population that had developed strong
national pride. It was unable to resist Bito conquest,
but it began to absorb Kimera's descendants more
thoroughly than had occurred elsewhere. The new
Bito dynasty spoke Luganda, the local language,
just as their kinsmen adopted the languages of each
kingdom they ruled. But they gradually lost their
Bito identity as each succeeding generation intermarried with the numerous powerful Baganda
clans. At some point in the nation's history the Bito
became so completely absorbed that even their
alien origin was ignored, and they regarded themselves, and were accepted by the local people, as
Baganda. In some Interlacustrine kingdoms the
Bito (like the Bahima and Watutsi farther south)
kept enough racial purity to be identifiable by their
great height and slenderness. In Buganda they
were absorbed racially as well.

This unique quality of Buganda to absorb its
conquering dynasty into its own society gave it a
high degree of internal unity and national pride.
About 1600 it stopped sending tribute to Bunyoro,
declaring itself an equally sovereign kingdom. Bunyoro launched a punitive campaign to brings its
rebellious vassal to heel, only to find that the Baganda stoutly defended their densely populated
homeland. Although the Banyoro were militarily
superior, they withdrew without seriously harming
Buganda, and the *Mukama* of Bunyoro concentrated his attention on other vassals.

For the next fifty years an uneasy peace was
maintained. Buganda was not strong enough to
attack Bunyoro, and Bunyoro was unwilling to attempt another invasion of Buganda. During this

time the *Kabakas* of Buganda slowly increased their kingdom's military strength. Then, in about 1650, Bunyoro launched a large-scale campaign against two of Buganda's neighbors, Ankole and Karagwe. Both kingdoms were strong enough to keep the Bunyoro army tied down, which encouraged Buganda to feel that it was safe to take the initiative. Baganda troops moved west, seized four small kingdoms on Buganda's border, and annexed them. Although these states were nominally vassals of Bunyoro, that kingdom was too busily engaged in its own campaigns to protest Buganda's expansionist move. By the time the Bunyoro war with Ankole and Karagwe had ended, Buganda was in solid control of its western acquisitions, too well entrenched to be dislodged. Buganda's area was now more than doubled, and its *Kabakas* wisely absorbed the new territories into the kingdom as counties rather than as subject states. By 1700 they were clearly and permanently part of Buganda, their royal families linked to leading Baganda clans by intermarriage, their chiefs ruling as appointees of the *Kabaka*.

Over the next century, between 1700 and 1800, Buganda slowly added new territories to its kingdom, moving cautiously west and east. Each new territory had been part of the Bunyoro feudal confederation, but Baganda troops avoided campaigning into Bunyoro's own homeland. By 1800 Buganda had again nearly doubled in size, and was by now larger in area and population than Bunyoro. In its two centuries of expansion Buganda followed a very different policy from that of Bunyoro, by moving slowly enough to incorporate its new territories fully and closely into the Buganda state. Within a few generations each new territory had become so closely linked with the state that its people accepted their membership in the Baganda nation as permanent. Buganda thus safeguarded itself against the frequent rebellions and acts of defiance that kept Bunyoro constantly engaged in military actions.

During these several centuries of growth neither Buganda nor Bunyoro is known to have engaged in any important long-distance trade. They were still largely isolated from developments on the Indian Ocean coast and in other parts of Africa. Around 1800, however, they and other Interlacustrine states began to participate in a growing commercial system with the Arab and Swahili traders along the coasts of Kenya and Tanzania. Arabs from Oman, in Arabia, had established a new government along the Indian Ocean coast of East Africa that was based in Zanzibar, and Swahili traders were cultivating commercial ties with a number of peoples in the western part of Tanzania. These peoples, among whom the Nyamwezi were especially prominent, served as middlemen in exchanging ivory, gold, slaves, and spices from the interior for guns, tools, weapons, and cloth from Arabia.

As this new trade system grew Buganda sought to dominate it in the southern and western parts of what is now Uganda. Bunyoro was unable to participate in it directly, since Buganda, Ankole, and Karagwe all lay closer to the main routes to the coast. Buganda's central position thus allowed its *Kabakas* to increase their wealth, while Bunyoro remained on the periphery of the commerce. By 1850 Buganda was encouraging Swahili agents to visit the kingdom and to establish trading stations, and a small number of guns began to filter in.

In the 1860's the first European explorers reached Buganda. Led by such British explorers as John Speke, Richard Burton, Samuel Baker, and James Grant, they had begun visiting the Interlacustrine Region late in the 1850's and were attracted by reports about Buganda, by now the most powerful kingdom in central Africa. When Speke, who was the first to reach the *Kabaka's* court, arrived, he was deeply impressed by the wealth, political organization, and power of that great kingdom.

The *Kabaka* at the time was Mutesa, one of the greatest of a long line. Described as a tall, handsome man with regal bearing and a majestic way of dealing with both his own people and visitors, Mutesa was respected far beyond the borders of his own kingdom. His capital, near the site of modern Kampala, was situated on a gently sloping hill, and miles of avenues bordered by plaited grass fences led toward the palace. The palace itself was a huge compound of grass houses, many as large as thirty or forty feet in diameter, gracefully built and laced with designs in their thatch walls. Within the compound were scores of these houses, in which lived the numerous wives of Mutesa and their children, his closest aides and advisers, and the royal servants. Nearby were barracks for more than a thousand men who served as Mutesa's personal guard and police force.

Into Mutesa's capital flowed immense quantities of grain, bananas, meat, and vegetables to feed the thousands of people who lived at court. Each day the *Kabaka* held audiences to hear the petitions and grievances of both nobles and commoners from many parts of the kingdom, since he served as chief judge as well as head of government. Buganda's *Kabaka*s, like most kings of Bantu Africa, were regarded as semidivine and were surrounded by nu-

Road to the
Kabaka's *palace*

Mutesa

merous taboos. By the nineteenth century the power of the *Kabakas* had become so great that they were held in dread and awe by their subjects. This power was checked only by the existence of a large and complex cabinet of ministers and title-holders, upon whom the *Kabaka* depended for advice and support.

For many decades after 1860 Britain regarded Buganda as the center of wealth and power for the interior of eastern Africa, and British missionaries and trade agents soon followed the explorers. French missionaries also worked in the kingdom in large numbers. Conversions to Christianity were numerous, especially among the nobility. By the 1880's there were thousands of devout Baganda Christians, divided into two powerful political factions. The Inglesa party represented the Protestants, most of whom had been converted by British missionaries, while the Fransa party represented the Catholics, who had ties with French Catholic missionaries. A third, smaller party represented the Muslims, who had been converted by the Swahili traders in the kingdom.

The long development of government and politics within Buganda had produced a state with a complex but efficient administration. All important officials were appointed by the *Kabaka*, and there was a chain of command leading from villages through districts and counties to the capital. The *Kabaka* maintained good government by a judicious balancing of political power among the many families and political factions. With the growth of the two Christian parties, who represented a majority of the most powerful families in the kingdom, it was necessary for the *Kabaka* to divide important offices among them so that neither felt discriminated against. In the late 1880's the two Christian parties united briefly to drive the Muslims from power, and afterward Buganda's internal affairs were dominated by the rival claims of these Christian factions. The *Kabaka* by that time was Mwanga, who was pro-Christian but carefully avoided becoming too closely identified with either the Catholics or Protestants.

In 1884, when the European scramble for African colonial conquest began, Germany announced to the world that it claimed East Africa. In effect this meant Tanganyika, but there was confusion for several years as to the extent of East Africa Germany was actually appropriating. In 1890 Germany and Britain signed an accord which gave Germany legal rights to Tanganyika, Rwanda, and Burundi (which were at the time called Ruanda-Urundi), and Britain rights to Kenya, Uganda, and Zanzibar. Since Britain regarded Buganda as by far the most important part of East Africa, British agents set to work to negotiate treaties with Kabaka Mwanga which would place Buganda under a British protectorate.

Mwanga generally welcomed the British presence, since it increased his access to trade, strengthened his military power internally, and gave him a powerful ally against Bunyoro. Bunyoro was still a strong state, and it had been actively expanding its power during the late nineteenth century into Busoga, on Buganda's east, and Ankole and Toro, on Buganda's west. Neither of these two leading kingdoms had attempted a serious invasion of the other's territory, but they were competing for possession of neighboring states.

In the competition between the two Britain sided completely with Buganda, and even accepted the argument put forward by Buganda that Bunyoro was a subordinate state. This was of course untrue, but Mwanga and his followers were clever enough to take advantage of Britain's great respect in order to exalt Buganda's position. Finally, in 1894, a large Baganda army marched against Bunyoro, with the support of British arms and ammunition and a small British military detachment. The well-equipped Baganda troops quickly defeated the Bunyoro army, drove a wedge through the center of the kingdom, and forced the *Mukama*, Kabarega, to flee. A peace treaty was later signed which allowed Kabarega to return to his throne, but it also gave Buganda control over the southwestern part of Bunyoro, as well as parts of Toro and Ankole.

This campaign was the last expansion that Buganda was able to undertake, but it ended with Buganda claiming most of what became southern

155

Uganda and controlling a territory that was many times larger than the kingdom had been in the past. Gradually British administrators extended British rule over the whole area, calling it Uganda (despite the fact that two-thirds of the country did not regard itself as part of Buganda) and giving the *Kabaka* a large measure of autonomy as a constitutional monarch.

During the colonial history of Uganda, from about 1900 to the 1960's, the British-supported expansion of Buganda proved to be a continuing source of political discontent in the country. The rulers of Ankole, Bunyoro, and Toro refused to acknowledge the *Kabaka's* claims to their territories seized during the 1894 war, and many other states within Uganda were jealous and fearful of Buganda's special, favored position. A few years after Uganda gained its independence from Britain in 1963 the *Kabaka*, Mutesa II, was stripped of his powers and exiled by the country's president. Tensions still continue between the Baganda and members of smaller states within Uganda, and the country's political affairs are deeply influenced by these tensions, as well as by continuing rivalry between Catholics and Protestants.

Buganda proved to be the most prominent and the best known of the great Interlacustrine kingdoms that the Bantu immigrants created. But it was, in fact, only one of many. Burundi, Rwanda, and scores of lesser known but impressive smaller kingdoms have covered the entire Interlacustrine area for more than six centuries, all attesting to the tremendous talent of the Bantu civilization for using effectively the environments into which its early pioneers moved. Within these prosperous kingdoms the arts flourished for centuries; sculptors modeled striking figures in clay and wood, poets created a vigorous tradition of poetry and oral literature, musicians devised and performed beautiful music, and the noble classes developed a graceful, cultivated way of life. With virtually no contact with the outside world before the nineteenth century, the Bantu civilization of the land between the lakes stands as one of the proudest and most brilliant accomplishments of an energetic, creative people.

7

The Swahili Civilization

Almost every part of Africa reached by the ancestors of the Bantu-speaking peoples was isolated from contact with the rest of the world until many centuries after Bantu settlement had taken place. One major, and fascinating, exception is the Indian Ocean coast of eastern Africa, where the Swahili civilization was destined to bloom as an offshoot of the basic Bantu civilization.

The Indian Ocean has been laced with maritime transportation routes for a very long period. As early as 2000 B.C. it was used by mariners to connect China, India, Indonesia, Persia, and Arabia with the northeastern lands of Africa, through the commercial system that flourished during the days of ancient Babylonia, Egypt, Greece, and Rome.

158

In the very earliest periods of the history of civilization canoes and ships manned by oarsmen skirted the shores on the northern rim of the Indian Ocean, carrying goods and curious adventurers. Mariners of China, Indonesia, India, and Arabia were the most skilled in the world in those ancient times, and it is from them that the Western world eventually learned the use of the compass, the astrolabe, and sails that enabled a ship to travel at angles into the wind rather than sailing only with the wind pushing it ahead.

How far south along the African coast these very ancient mariners voyaged is unknown. The ancient Greek historian Herodotus reported that a small Phoenician fleet circumnavigated the whole African continent around 700 or 600 B.C., but this feat has never been proved. Even earlier, however, Egyptian and Babylonian ships had traded frequently with each other, rowing and sailing through the Red Sea, the Gulf of Aden, the northern edge of the Indian Ocean, and the Persian Gulf. Egyptian ships are known from written records to have visited the land of Punt, which was probably located in Somalia near the southern end of the Red Sea, as early as 1500 B.C. Although they left no record of voyages farther south in Africa, it is reasonable to assume that they occasionally ventured down the African coast, either purposefully or accidentally.

During all these centuries when ships from the ancient civilizations may have visited the shores of eastern Africa, no records were left to indicate what they found, or indeed if they sailed there at all. A certain amount of archeological work has been done along the coasts of Kenya and Tanzania, but it has turned up no clues to ancient African contacts with the civilizations to the north and east. All that is sure is that the Indian Ocean was a familiar sea to mariners. The ancient Greeks called it the Erythraean Sea, and it is clearly marked on Herodotus' map of the world, drawn in about 430 B.C.

The first definite record of contact between the northern world and eastern Africa comes from a mariner's guide called the *Periplus of the Erythraean Sea,* which was written about A.D. 60. Its unknown author gives sailing directions, information about ports, and data on goods to be traded in East Africa, describing river mouths, islands, and land features as far south as present-day Tanzania. Only a few years before the *Periplus* was written a Greek merchant named Hippalus had described an important geographic fact that had long been known in Asia but was novel to the Greeks and Romans: the regular annual appearance of the monsoon winds of the Indian Ocean, which blow steadily from the southwest between May and October, shifting between November and March to blow from the northeast. Ships using the monsoons could sail swiftly and easily down the East African coast between November and March, then back between May and October.

The *Periplus* said that the first port to be gained after rounding Cape Guardafui, the tip of Somalia, was Opone, where one could obtain cinnamon, tortoise shell, and slaves. It then mentioned islands which were reached after many days of sailing along barren coasts. These were probably the is-
160

lands of the Lamu archipelago off the coast of northern Kenya. Fifteen days further south, it said, there is an island named Menuthias, which was probably Zanzibar or its neighbor, Pemba. Two days further one came to the large market town of Rhapta, which is believed to have been near the mouth of Tanzania's Rufiji River.

All the coastal lands of East Africa were called Azania by the Greeks, and the *Periplus* described the Azanians as "men of piratical habits, and of very great size." Rhapta and other points were ruled by Arabs, according to the *Periplus,* "who live together with the people of [Azania] and inter-marry with them, and who know the area and understand their language."

Several significant points emerge from a careful study of the *Periplus*. First, the coastlands of East Africa were at least sparsely settled before A.D. 100, and were definitely involved in trade with the great civilizations of the Mediterranean and Asia. Second, Arabs were already settled at several com-mercial centers on the East African coast and were extensively intermarried with the local inhabitants. Third, the "piratical" men "of very great size" were very probably not the early Bantu settlers. Not only are the coastal Bantu peoples not of particularly great size, but Greeks writing at that time would have called attention to Negroid physical features had the ancient Azanians been as Negroid as the early Bantu settlers.

The earliest settlers of the East African coast were southern Cushites, related to the Cushites from farther north who had settled in the Great Rift Valley in East Africa's interior. They were tall,

161

Cushite warriors

and their skins were brown rather than black. Their facial features would have been sharper and less Negroid than those of the Bantu immigrants. Since they were related to the Ethiopians and Somalis, they probably had no physical features that the Greeks would have called attention to, other than their height.

Within a very few centuries after the writing of the *Periplus,* however, this situation had changed. Small families of Bantu-speaking pioneers pressed northward along the coast from Mozambique and settled the entire territory as far north as the present area of Mogadiscio in Somalia. There are several vague references in Greek, Byzantine, and even Chinese writings to East Africa, which by that time was called Zanj, from an Arab word meaning "black." In the early tenth century a great Arabic scholar, al-Masudi, wrote a treatise on geography in which he described much of the East African coast and its Zanj peoples. In al-Masudi's

162

time these ancestors of the Bantu had apparently absorbed the earlier Cushites, had intermarried with the colonies of Arabs just as the Cushites had done, and had helped to create a number of market towns dotting the coast as far south as Sofala in Mozambique.

The Zanj, as al-Masudi told of them, had created a large kingdom covering much of the East African coast, and their king ruled from Sofala. Many were Muslims, although there were numerous "idolators" on the coast and in the interior. From the Zanj land came large quantities of highly prized leopard skins, tortoise shell, ivory, and gold, as well as a steady supply of slaves for the markets of Arabia and India. Al-Masudi notes that the ivory of East Africa was shipped primarily to India and China, where it was used for making thrones, dagger and sword handles, sword scabbards, chessmen, and backgammon pieces. He notes that the Zanj used cattle both for food and for beasts of burden, and that they were accomplished ironworkers. Their language he described as "elegant," and he was highly impressed by the many orators who spoke eloquently to the people on morality and religion.

In the earlier days of trade along East Africa's coasts the main exports were tortoise shell, ivory, coconut products, fish, and other products that were available on or near the coast itself. By the tenth century, when al-Masudi wrote, all these goods were still important, but ivory had become a much larger item in the trade. To the list of goods had been added gold and fine leopard skins. The expansion of ivory exports, and the addition

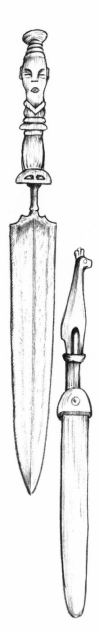

Ivory-handled swords

163

of gold and leopard skins, indicates that goods were now flowing from a larger interior region to commercial centers along the coast. Sofala, far to the south, was apparently the main commercial center, and we know from studying the history of central Africa that the Rhodesian plateau's goods reached the outside world through Sofala.

The coast of eastern Africa is relatively fertile between southern Mozambique and northern Kenya, although the Somali coast is barren except for a few points where rivers flowing into the sea create restricted fertile areas. Behind the fertile coastal strip, in northern Mozambique, Tanzania, and Kenya, there is a wide belt of semiarid country. Since this inhospitable belt separated the coastal peoples of East Africa from their prosperous relatives in the interior Interlacustrine Region, whatever wealth the coastal peoples could accumulate had to come from maritime trade, from the access to the interior in Mozambique, and from trading with the primitive hunters and food-gatherers who for many centuries were the only inhabitants of the dry inland belt.

This basic fact of geography underlay the origin and development of the Swahili civilization which dominated the coasts of eastern Africa from about A.D. 1000 up to modern times. Its peoples interacted with each other rather than with their relatives in the interior, and they looked to the sea for trade and ideas. At strategic points along the coastal mainland and on the myriad fertile islands that lie just offshore they created commercial centers, each connected with the other by a system of trade. Into these centers came ships from Arabia, India, and

164

THE SWAHILI COAST c. 1500

Lake Rudolf

Lake Kyoga

(SOMALIA)

Mogadiscio

Brava

(UGANDA)

(KENYA)

Kismayu

Lake Victoria Nyanza

Pate

Lamu

Malindi

Mombasa

(TANZANIA)

Pemba

Zanzibar

Bagamoyo

Indian Ocean

Mafia

Kilwa

Lindi

COMORO IS.

Lake Nyasa

(MOZAMBIQUE)

(MALAWI)

Mozambique I.

Mozambique Channel

Quelimane

MADAGASCAR

Sofala

Louise E. Jefferson

China, to exchange beads, fine tools and weapons, silks, cotton cloth, glass bottles, porcelain vessels, and jewelry for the gold, iron, animal skins, shell, ivory, beeswax, honey, spices, and slaves that the coastal merchants collected from the long coastal belt and from the hinterland.

The Arabs, sailing down from the Red Sea and the Arabian Gulf, were involved in this trading system for more than two thousand years. Between the seventh and tenth centuries Arab involvement was overshadowed by Persian control of the sea, and between the sixteenth and eighteenth centuries the Portuguese severely curtailed Arab activity. But apart from those two interludes, Arabs have long been the most constant visitors to the East African coast.

Arabs, as we have seen, were calling at points along the East African coast and intermarrying with the settlements of Cushites even before the first Bantu-speaking peoples arrived. When the Bantu speakers began to settle the coast, they quickly absorbed the Cushite and Arab-Cushite peoples there and became the predominant people. They did not, however, reject the continuing influx of Arab merchants and settlers, nor the ideas these men brought. They seem to have accepted the Arab contact as natural and desirable, since it provided a lucrative channel of communication with the non-African world.

The Bantu immigrants settled a two-thousand-mile coastline within a few centuries, stopping in Somalia only when they encountered the desert and the pastoral Somali and Galla peoples who lived there. In this period they gradually developed

166

new dialects and languages, and their widely dispersed populations eventually evolved into separate ethnic groups. There were two influences, however, that prevented this process from producing a new group of Bantu peoples who were sharply divided among themselves. The continuing influx of Arabs, with the Islamic religion and the Arabic language, was one force which affected all alike. The second was the concentration on the sea and maritime pursuits. The East African coastal Bantu peoples were accomplished sailors, and their boats helped to keep each group in touch with others.

The result was the gradual development of the Swahili civilization, which gave the Bantu peoples over an immensely long territory a common language, a common religion, continuing contact with each other, and a common culture.

Interestingly enough there is no tribe which can properly be called "the Swahili." Swahili is a Bantu language, obviously related to the languages of the peoples on the Rhodesian plateau, in Katanga, and in the Interlacustrine Region. But it has absorbed a number of Arabic words (and, in more recent times, words from English and German) and has been adopted by hundreds of separate ethnic groups in eastern Africa. The many coastal peoples who speak the language live in very much the same way, so that their culture is often described as a "Swahili culture." Some, especially those on the coasts of Kenya and Tanzania, long ago stopped speaking any other Bantu language, and adopted Swahili as their mother tongue. It is no longer clear where the Swahili language originated, except somewhere along the East African coast, although

167

its deepest imprint seems to be along the Tanzania coast.

Somali woman

Although al-Masudi does not use the term "Swahili" to describe either the people or the language along the East African coast, it is clear from his descriptions of them that the blend between Bantu and Arab had already begun to lay the foundation for the development of the Swahili civilization. Four centuries later another great Arabic scholar visited East Africa and wrote of the Swahili, at a time when their civilization had bloomed into a graceful, urban culture based on trade with the countries bordering the Indian Ocean.

This second great Arabic scholar was Ibn-Battuta, whose descriptions of East Africa provide us with delightfully clear and accurate accounts of the people and their way of life. Ibn-Battuta was an African himself, born in Tangier, Morocco, in 1304, and dying in Marrakesh, Morocco, in 1377. He was a brilliant, well-educated scholar and lawyer, who practiced Islamic law in many parts of North Africa and Asia Minor. Early in his life he acquired great curiosity and a love of travel, and he devoted much of his life to satisfying this curiosity by going on long voyages to the farthest corners of the known world.

Ibn-Battuta was a gifted writer and a careful observer. As he traveled to new lands he kept notes on the people, their houses, their foods, their clothing, their commerce, their religion, their rulers and prominent people, and other points of interest. Later in his life he published accounts of his travels, and his works were so sound that he is today one of the most important references for

168

scholars studying the world of the fourteenth century. Ibn-Battuta has been compared with Marco Polo, who traveled and wrote less than a century earlier. But Battuta was superior to Polo in many respects: he traveled far more widely, was better educated, and wrote more accurate and detailed accounts of his findings.

Battuta visited East Africa in 1331, at a time when the Swahili civilization was at its zenith. He visited the three greatest cities on the coast: Mogadiscio in Somalia, Mombasa in Kenya, and Kilwa in Tanzania, as well as several smaller towns. His descriptions paint a picture of prosperity and civilized life, although he found some of the smaller towns quite unpleasant because of the odors from their slaughterhouses and fisheries.

Mogadiscio, said Battuta, was "a very large town," whose people "have very many camels, and slaughter many hundreds every day." "The merchants," he wrote, "are wealthy, and manufacture a material [probably fine leather] which takes its name from the town and which is exported to Egypt and elsewhere." Mogadiscio, like all the East African towns and cities, was ruled by a sultan, whom the local people called *sheikh,* and its peoples, whom Battuta noted were black, were Muslims. The leading *qadi,* or Islamic legal expert and judge, was Battuta's host, and Battuta found that he was followed wherever he went by a large group of students of law and religion. These students, hoping to become *qadis* themselves, were housed in a specially built house, located near the *sheikh's* palace, which was "decorated with carpets and contained everything needful."

A sheikh

Battuta described the food of Mogadiscio's people, which was typical of the diet of most of the coast, as "rice cooked with butter, served on a large wooden dish. With it they serve side-dishes, stews of chicken, meat, fish, and vegetables." These basic foods were accompanied at each meal by pickles and spices, "[cooked] unripe bananas in fresh milk . . . as a sauce," and "curdled milk . . . with peppercorns, vinegar, and saffron, green ginger and mangoes."

On Battuta's first Friday in the city, when it was time for the prayers at the mosque, his host brought him clothes from the *sheikh*'s palace so that he could go to prayer dressed in the same way as the leading men of Mogadiscio. "Their dress consists of a loin-cloth, which they fastened round the waist . . . a tunic of Egyptian linen with a border, a cloak of Jerusalem stuff, doubled, and a fringed turban of Egyptian material."

Mogadiscio's *sheikh* was a man of great dignity, and was treated with deep respect by the city's people. He frequently walked through the city to the mosque, accompanied by hundreds of servants, aides, military commanders, legal experts, and government officials. After Friday prayers the *sheikh* held court, where he reviewed legal questions that were too important to be decided by the *qadi*, or the *wazirs* and *amirs*, the senior officials who sat together as a high court. All questions to the *sheikh* were put to him in writing, and he wrote his decision on the back of the paper so that the paper became an official, legal record.

Ibn-Battuta found Mogadiscio to be a pleasant, civilized city, with a dignified system of govern-

170

ment and law and a teeming economy. He was even more impressed by Kilwa, however, which was the southernmost city of consequence on the East African coast.

Kilwa was built on an island which was only a few hundred yards off the coast of southern Tanzania. Battuta noted that it was "in the land of the Swahili . . . in the land of Zanj." He described it as "the principal town on the coast, the greater part of whose inhabitants are Zanj of very black complexion." It was, he found, "one of the most beautiful and well-constructed towns in the world. The whole of it is elegantly built. The roofs are built with mangrove poles. There is very much rain. The people are engaged in a holy war, for their country lies beside that of the pagan Zanj. The chief qualities are devotion and piety. . . ."

Kilwa's importance was due to its command of the flow of African goods out of central and southern Africa into the Indian Ocean commercial system. Although Sofala, which Battuta placed at

Ruins of mosque, Kilwa

"half a month's march from Kilwa," was the point at which the goods arrived at the seacoast, they were then shipped up to Kilwa for sale to the fleets of large ships that came from Arabia, India, and China. It is also likely that there was a steady flow of African goods from the inland country around Lakes Tanganyika and Malawi to Kilwa, but little is known of the routes used or which inland peoples brought them to the coast.

Into Kilwa's great anchorage sailed many ships, even though it was the southernmost port on Africa's Indian Ocean coast. In its ruins archeologists have found tens of thousands of bits and pieces of fine glass, porcelain, and pottery from Arabia, India, and China, as well as thousands of coins from these lands. Most of the ships entering Kilwa were Arab ships, although it is possible that Chinese ships may have visited there on occasion.

Great fleets of Chinese vessels are known from Chinese records to have put in at Mogadiscio, at Brava, just south of it, and at Malindi in Kenya during the early fifteenth century, but there are scattered references to voyages to East Africa dating back as early as the ninth century. The Chinese were far in advance of other peoples in their naval skills; they were using the compass at least as early as the tenth century, and were building great ships as long as three hundred feet, with three masts and five layers of decks. One Chinese fleet under Admiral Cheng Po, which visited East Africa in 1417–19 and again in 1431, is thought to have been manned by more than twenty thousand men.

During the thirteenth century the sultan of Kilwa established a mint, which cast and stamped Kilwa coins for use both in the city and along the Swahili coast. The only other East African city-states which are known to have minted their own coins are Zanzibar and Mogadiscio.

Between 1300 and 1500 the Swahili civilization reached its highest peak of development. There were during that period at least sixty sizable towns and cities along the coast which were regular ports of call for large ships, and scores of smaller towns which were connected with the major centers by frequent sailings of small coastwise ships. The most important cities were Brava, Kismayu, and Mogadiscio in Somalia; Lamu, Pate, Malindi, Mombasa, and Vumba Kuu in Kenya; and Bagamoyo, Zanzibar, Mafia, and Kilwa in Tanzania. The cities of Somalia had by this time been brought under the political rule and cultural dominance of Somali chieftains, who created a number of sultanates. They still had Bantu settlers living in them, and Swahili was known by many of the inhabitants, but the Somali language and Arabic were more important.

From Pate and Lamu south, however, Swahili was the main language spoken both at home and at court, although all the noble and wealthy peoples knew Arabic. Literacy in Arabic was common among the wealthy, but by the fifteenth or sixteenth century, if not earlier, a written form of Swahili had been developed as well. A few centuries later, during the 1700's, a great tradition of Swahili writing had appeared, with local intellectuals writing poetry, history, and works on religion, morality, philosophy, and government.

The Swahili political system was based on the sultanate, with a sultan ruling a city and the territory surrounding it. At various points in the histories of each city fresh groups of Arab immigrants arrived, accompanied by well-armed marines, and established their rule over the city-states. Invariably they married local women, however, so that within a few generations the ruling line was a clearly Swahili line. The Swahili sultans were considered local people, not aliens, and traced their descent both through their Arab and their African ancestors. They spoke Swahili and were guided by local tradition in their manners and customs. They were devout Muslims, as were virtually all Swahili and Arabs, and most made the required pilgrimage to Mecca to pray at the holy shrine there.

The political life of the Swahili city-states was complicated both by frequent local intrigue and by conflicts between the cities. Since each city was sovereign, and had a vital interest in the trade which linked it with all the others, it was often at odds with other cities. Small-scale wars were common, as were temporary alliances between two or more cities when threatened by another. Within each city there were families and political factions which competed for favored position with the sul-

174

tan. Close ties to the sultan gave a group access to high and lucrative political offices, such as customs collector, and better trading opportunities.

When sultans were just and politically skillful, they were able to maintain tranquillity in their city with ease. But unjust or inept sultans found themselves at odds with powerful families. There are many instances of civil strife during the reigns of unpopular sultans, and some sultans were deposed by strong factions in order that a more popular or just member of the royal line could be placed on the throne. During Ibn-Battuta's visit the sultan of Kilwa was one of that city's greatest and most revered, Abu al-Muzaffar Hasan, who was called by his people "The Father of Gifts" because of his great charity. Many stories were told Battuta of Hasan's generosity to beggars and the poor of Kilwa, and his people praised his deep piety and concern for their welfare. Battuta notes, however, that this great and beloved sultan was succeeded, when he died, by a brother, Daud, who was just the opposite: stingy, harsh, and unpopular.

The early visit of al-Masudi and the later visit of Ibn-Battuta provide clear and valuable firsthand accounts of life in the developing cities of the Swahili civilization. Archeologists have begun excavations in a number of ruined sites, and have found the crumbling remains of once-beautiful buildings, along with the myriad pieces of debris that were left by a civilized people over a period of a thousand years. Yet for the past few centuries the great cities of the Swahili have been nearly dead. Some were abandoned, gradually to disappear under the attacks of weather and pillagers. Others declined to

Swahili man

sleepy towns populated by fishermen and petty traders. The decline of this once-great civilization is a story in its own right. And once again, it was the impact of the Portuguese which created conditions under which the Swahili civilization found it impossible to maintain its former greatness.

The first Portuguese visitors to the coasts of East Africa arrived at the very end of the fifteenth century, when Vasco da Gama and his fleet of four caravels rounded the Cape of Good Hope and began sailing north in 1498. All the Portuguese voyages before that of Da Gama had explored the western coasts of Africa; Da Gama's great feat was to sail directly southeast from the westernmost tip of Africa in Senegal until he reached the Cape of Good Hope, thereby greatly reducing the sailing time to the Indian Ocean. Vasco da Gama was not interested in careful exploration of Africa. His mission was twofold: to locate the legendary kingdom of Prester John, thought to be in Ethiopia, and to chart the most direct sea route to India. After he rounded the Cape he sailed north, touching at several points without lengthy stops for exploration, then set sail across the northern edge of the Indian Ocean to reach India itself.

In his first few stops in eastern Africa, Da Gama found fierce, cattle-herding peoples who were not impressive to his crew. They did not seem to possess obvious wealth. Finally, however, in the Mozambique Channel between Madagascar and the mainland he began finding settled towns, then the great trading centers of the Swahili civilization. At one of his earliest landings he visited the town of Quilimane, and was surprised to find "Moors," as the Portuguese called all dark-skinned Muslims from Africa, who were well dressed, haughty, and somewhat disdainful of the Portuguese. The farther north he sailed the more evidence he found of a people whose civilization was fully as advanced as that of the Portuguese. Although Da Gama expected these people to be awed by his vessels, they quickly assured him that they frequently saw much larger and more impressive ships, although they came from the north, from Arabia and India, rather than from the south.

As soon as Da Gama returned to Portugal, his countrymen realized they had found access to their long-sought goals. By finding a faster route around Africa, they could now sail to India without fear of the hostile Muslim powers of the eastern Mediterranean, who had for centuries stood between Europe and the wealth of the Far East. By learning that sailing conditions were excellent along Africa's East Coast, they knew that they had come much closer to locating Prester John, whose support they believed might be helpful against the Arabs, Persians, and Turks. And Da Gama's reports of highly developed, civilized cities and a thriving commercial system along the coastline of eastern Africa offered an opportunity, hitherto unsuspected, to acquire wealth and booty from East Africa itself.

In the twenty-five years following Da Gama's voyage, Portugal sent more than two hundred ships to East Africa. Since Portugal was a small, poor nation and the building, equipping, and manning of ships a great expense, it is clear that East Africa was regarded as worth considerable investment.

177

The records left by the Portuguese chroniclers of the sixteenth century show just as clearly that this investment paid off. Portuguese ships seized large stores of gold, ivory, spices, silks, and coins in many of the Swahili cities; Portuguese forts were built along the Mozambique coast to serve as bases for a Portuguese naval force; and Portuguese fleets occupied several of the more prosperous cities in order to control the trade entering and leaving their harbors.

The history of the Portuguese adventure in East Africa is a sad story of plunder and brutality. Official documents show that Portugal's objectives were completely mercenary and that its commanders were authorized to use any means they chose to seize East African wealth. Sultans who resisted were exiled or executed. Nobles and officials who lied or failed to carry out Portuguese orders were tortured, maimed, or killed. Portuguese fleets sailed into peaceful East African harbors, trained their guns on the graceful buildings, and leveled them with heavy bombardments. Mombasa, which refused to acknowledge Portuguese authority, was almost completely destroyed in 1505 by a large fleet under the command of Francisco de Almeida. When the sultan, who had fled with his retainers, returned to the charred ruins of his city, he wrote a letter to the sultan of Malindi in which he reported that he found "no living thing in it, neither man nor woman, young nor old, nor child however little. All who had failed to escape had been killed and burned."

Brava, then the second largest city in Somalia, was sacked at about the same time, when its sultan resisted Portuguese occupation. A Portuguese writer who was present wrote that Brava "was destroyed by the Portuguese, who slew many of its peoples and carried them into captivity, and took great spoil of gold and silver and goods."

Under the Portuguese onslaught a few Swahili cities prospered, at least at first, for their sultans welcomed the Europeans as allies against other sultans. Malindi, which was at war with Mombasa in 1498, gave Vasco da Gama a most cordial welcome and solicited his help in its cause. Yet even the cities which were friendly to the Portuguese soon learned that their new "allies" had only one real purpose, to enrich themselves as quickly and easily as possible. Rebellions were common throughout the sixteenth century, even in the friendliest cities, as their rulers, merchants, and commoners found their livelihoods threatened by the Portuguese stranglehold.

The Portuguese found the conquest of most Swahili cities relatively easy. Guns were not in common use in East Africa, and warfare, though frequent, was a minor pursuit for the commercial peoples of the Swahili civilization. Before the coming of the Portuguese, war had been a matter of a few ships, with a few hundred men armed with swords, lances, and bows battling each other until one side or the other capitulated. Each of these small wars soon ended with few casualties and little destruction, and life quickly returned to normal. For the Portuguese, however, war was a deadly serious business. Their aim was to seize whatever goods of value they could find, then crush potential opposition so that new wealth would flow only into Portuguese hands.

The Portuguese ships were armed with cannon,

and the men wore iron breastplates, helmets, and armor. Well armed with noisy arquebuses, long swords, axes, and sharp-studded maces, the Portuguese soldiers were well trained, tightly disciplined, and fiercely motivated. Every expedition sailed with the knowledge and approval of the Portuguese throne, and was blessed by the Portuguese Catholic Church's highest officials. From the throne came plain orders to subject the rulers of East Africa to Portuguese control and to return with their wealth. From the Church came orders to stamp out Islam and to spread Christianity under the Portuguese banner. Success in the expeditions led to large amounts of booty, often enough to allow a soldier to live out his life in prosperous retirement, and warm praise from Crown and Church. Cowardice and failure were punished.

All this helped to make the Portuguese naval captains and their men bold and aggressive. The glittering wealth they found in East Africa was in the hands of hated Muslims, against whom Portugal had struggled for centuries. Even the Church expressed little criticism if cruelty and harshness

180

were used in the holy mission of conquest and conversion of Muslim infidels.

Portuguese captains from Da Gama's second expedition on were given explicit instructions for handling the sultans of the Swahili cities. Each was to be approached peacefully and told to submit to the sovereignty of the king of Portugal. Portuguese chaplains, military officers, and commercial agents were to be comfortably established in each city to insure that the sultan ruled in the manner required by Portugal. Taxes and customs duties were to be paid to Portugal. But, the instructions noted, the Portuguese captains were to make it clear that force could and would be used if the sultans refused to accept the Portuguese terms. The captains were authorized to bombard cities, send troops ashore, take hostages or slaves, and even, if they felt it desirable, sack a city and seize all wealth they found in it.

The Portuguese, both in Lisbon and on the warships, were quite aware that these merciless policies were directed at a civilized people. They were under no illusion that the Swahili were savages. Their ships had educated men aboard, and many kept detailed notes that were published as official chronicles in Lisbon. These chronicles, in fact, written in the first few decades of the Portuguese adventure in East Africa, provide us with the best accounts of the cities that the Portuguese impoverished and destroyed.

The chronicle of Vasco da Gama's first expedition paints a gracious picture of Malindi, whose sultan at first welcomed the Portuguese and signed an alliance with them. "Malindi lies in a bay," it says,

181

"and extends along the shore. It may be likened to Alcouchette [a Portuguese town near Lisbon]. Its houses are lofty and well white-washed, and have many windows; on the land side are palm groves, and all around it maize and vegetables are being cultivated."

Kilwa was of course a larger, richer, and more impressive city. In 1500 the chronicle of a ship under the command of Captain Pedro Cabral called it "a beautiful country. The houses are high like those of Spain. In this land there are rich merchants, and there is much gold and silver and amber and musk and pearls. Those of the land wear clothes of fine cotton and of silk and many fine things, and they are black men."

The best description left of Kilwa was written, ironically enough, by a chronicler with the large fleet of Admiral Francisco de Almeida, which was sent in 1505–6 to subjugate Kilwa and other cities that had refused to accept the Portuguese yoke. At that time, the chronicle relates, Kilwa "was mistress of Mombasa, Melinde [Malindi], the islands of Pemba, Zanzibar, Monfia [Mafia], Comoro, and many other settlements which rose from the power and wealth it acquired after becoming sovereign of the mine of Sofala. . . ." In the city itself "the greater number of the houses are built of stone and mortar, with flat roofs, and at the back there are orchards planted with fruit trees and palms to give shade and please the sight as well as for their fruit. . . . At one part of the town the king had his palace, built in the style of a fortress, with towers and turrets and every kind of defense, with a door opening to the quay to allow of en-

182

trance from the sea, and another large door on the side of the fortress that opened on the town. From our ships the fine houses, terraces, and minarets, with the palms and trees in the orchards, made the city look so beautiful that our men were eager to land and overcome the pride of this barbarian, who spent all that night in bringing into the island archers from the mainland."

Admiral de Almeida's fleet, with fifteen warships and nearly a thousand troops, was well equipped to handle even the fortress-like palace of Kilwa's sultan. He landed five hundred men at dawn, heavily armored and armed, and stormed the palace. Several hours of bloody fighting were needed before Kilwa's soldiers were forced to retreat, but by that time the sultan and his court had escaped to the mainland, safely out of De Almeida's reach. Following the capitulation of the city, De Almeida's first official act was to organize looting parties, and his second was to install a new sultan who was willing to accept Portuguese sovereignty.

The Portuguese found the immediate plunder of

183

such cities as Kilwa highly profitable, since the many wealthy Swahili merchants and nobles owned large stores of gold, ivory, gems, and fine imports from the Far East. The business of maintaining the plunder of the coast's wealth, however, proved to be another problem entirely.

Almost as soon as Portuguese governors and agents were settled in the Swahili cities, the supplies of gold and ivory from the interior began to diminish. Anti-Portuguese Swahili traders used their substantial influence with the peoples of Rhodesia and other interior lands to persuade them to stop sending goods to the coast, where they would fall into Portuguese hands. Within a few decades, by 1550, the bustling commercial system of East Africa had dwindled to an unimportant trickle of goods.

The Portuguese themselves helped to destroy East Africa's commerce by diverting the trade with India and China directly to Europe. With few goods reaching the ports of East Africa, neither the interior peoples nor the Swahili traders had any incentive to produce. Except for a few spots where the Portuguese were able to trade directly with the interior, such as in Mwene Mutapa, they soon found that their East African prize was of far less value than it had at first appeared. By 1600 their main interests in eastern Africa were in holding it against Muslim reconquest from the north and in establishing several bases which Portuguese ships could use as way-stations on their way to and from the Far East. The main base of the Portuguese was on Mozambique Island, where they built a fortress and established a military and government

184

Fort Jesus, Mombasa

post. In 1594 they built a second strong bastion at
Fort Jesus, in Mombasa, which served as a base for
the Portuguese ships that were busy putting
down revolts in the Swahili cities and preventing
Arab ships from sailing in East African waters.

Portugal found it necessary to maintain substantial garrisons in Mozambique, Mombasa, and the
other occupied Swahili cities and towns. As the
coastal trade dwindled, these outposts of Portuguese empire eventually became more costly to
maintain than the revenues they were supposed to
protect. Yet Portugal, still clinging to her dream of
being a great imperial power, held on tenaciously.
Almost every year there was an uprising or rebellion in one or another of the conquered Swahili
towns, for the Portuguese were deeply resented.
And in the last few decades of the sixteenth century, Arab ships, backed by the power of Turkey's
mushrooming Ottoman Empire, began to venture
with increasing boldness into East African waters.
It was to guard against them that the great fortress
at Mombasa was built, but even that bastion eventually proved unequal to the task.

185

Portugal continued to cling stubbornly to its rebellious and unprofitable possessions in East Africa throughout the seventeenth century, but the chief result was to continue the sad stagnation that Portuguese rule had created. Those towns and cities that had not been destroyed sank gradually into deeper poverty and apathy, their people resentful of Portuguese control but not strong enough to oust their hated overlords. By about 1650 the entire East African coast had declined so badly that the once-great mosques, palaces, and public buildings were abandoned and falling apart. Only the small areas occupied by the Portuguese, and supported by Portuguese money, were able to maintain some semblance of civilization.

In 1694 a fleet of Arab ships from the sultanate of Oman, on the southeastern corner of the Arabian peninsula, defeated the Portuguese defenders of Mombasa and ejected the last of the Portuguese from Fort Jesus. Portuguese power in East Africa was dead, except far to the south, along the coast of Mozambique.

With the expulsion of the Portuguese, both the Arab conquerors and the Swahili attempted to revive the ancient trade that had brought such prosperity. Their efforts were never fully successful, however, because the gold and ivory of Mozambique and Rhodesia, which had been the most important exports, were still cut off by the Portuguese in Mozambique. Not until the late eighteenth century was a measure of prosperity revived, when Arab and Swahili traders managed to establish economic ties with the interior of East Africa itself. Gradually a new flow of goods began to reach

Kilwa, Zanzibar, Bagamoyo, and Mombasa, and the most important part of the flow consisted of slaves.

The growth of this new trading system was due, in part, to the efforts of Britain and other countries to end the slave trade between West Africa and the New World. It was also stimulated by the development of a new market for slaves on the Indian Ocean islands of Mauritius, Réunion, and Madagascar, which had imported very few slaves before the late eighteenth century. The French were busy colonizing Mauritius and Réunion, both of which had unusually fertile soil and were capable of producing substantial amounts of sugar. On Madagascar wealthy aristocrats among the ruling Merina and Sakalava peoples were seeking slaves to till their lands and herd their cattle.

The Omani Arabs, having driven the Portuguese out of East Africa, concentrated their attention on establishing their own rule there, and in this they were successful. Late in the eighteenth century all the Swahili cities were occupied, with small colonies of Omani Arabs as ruling groups. In 1834 the sultan of Oman moved his court to Zanzibar, and from this new base created a loosely knit empire that stretched all along the coasts of Kenya and Tanzania. Gradually the Zanzibar sultans pressed their influence into the interior of East Africa, penetrating as far as Zaire and the Interlacustrine kingdoms. But their influence was more commercial than political, even though they were able to send formidable forces of Arab and Swahili troops, well armed with guns, into the interior to seize slaves and punish chiefs who refused to trade with them.

187

Possibly the Omani rulers of East Africa would have been fully absorbed into the Swahili society, as Arabs had been for the past two thousand years, had the European colonial conquest not introduced a new element into the situation. But in the period 1884–1900 East Africa was divided up into German and British spheres, and the sultan of Zanzibar became a monarch of limited power. The twentieth century brought new ideas and new forces under European colonial rule, and the Swahili emerged into the modern period of independence viewing both the British and the Arabs as alien conquerors.

In the new nations of East Africa the Swahili people are a minority, since they are now only a part of larger states which include the Interlacustrine peoples as well as those who live in the middle lands of the interior. The Swahili language, however, has been adopted by so many peoples in the interior that it is the official language of Tanzania and is widely spoken in Kenya and Uganda. The Swahili have contributed their language, rich in poetry and philosophy, to the process which is developing a wholly new civilization in East Africa by blending many elements of African culture with that of Europe.

Drakensberg Mountains

8

Shaka Zulu and
the Tormented Land

Of all the great thrusts of Bantu expansion, that into the southern tip of the African continent was the latest and slowest. And more than any other, it was the one destined to offer the Bantu-speaking peoples their cruelest challenges and their most poignant tragedies.

The movement of Bantu-speaking peoples onto the Rhodesian plateau was rapid, but to the south of that land lay increasingly harsh country, which rarely offered fertile soil and comfortable climate. And the southern lands, ill-suited as they were to the agricultural pursuits of the migrating Bantu peoples, were already widely settled by earlier peoples of the ancient Khoisan language family who

189

hunted wild animals and tended herds for their livelihood.

The territory that now includes the powerful Republic of South Africa, Botswana, Lesotho, Namibia, and Swaziland offers a wide range of geographical conditions. Much of it is high and cool: The central plateau of South Africa is often 6,000 feet and more above sea level, and its southerly latitude brings winter conditions of low temperatures and chilling winds. Great expanses of desert lie to the south and west of the South African plateau. The Kalahari Desert, which covers much of Namibia, is the second largest in Africa after the Sahara, and the smaller Namib Desert is one of the driest, least hospitable regions on earth.

Many parts of Botswana, Namibia, and western South Africa consist of vast dry plains which lie at lower altitudes than the central plateau. These plains are excessively hot in summer and cold in winter, and the rains that fall on them are light, seasonal, and unpredictable. They will support only the barest minimum of grain cultivation, with very low yields per acre. Although cattle and wild game can live on their tough wild grasses, periods of drought every few years take a high toll of animal life.

East of the South African central plateau stretches a high chain of peaks, the Drakensberg Mountains, that rises to more than 10,000 feet above sea level and serves as a giant barrier between the central plateau and the lowlands near the Indian Ocean. In these lowlands the ancient Bantu farmers found good conditions for their agriculture. There the climate is warm or mild the
190

year round, and rainfall is relatively abundant and regular. Only the far tip of South Africa, around modern Cape Town, offers a comparably benign environment, but that small territory was nearly 1,000 miles from the main centers of Bantu settlement, and the drier lands in between were the homelands of the Khoisan cattle herders.

Where the southern African environment offered a reasonable opportunity, the ancestors of the Bantu-speaking peoples moved in early. From archeological evidence they are known to have established themselves in the northern part of the province of Transvaal, south of the Limpopo River, as early as the ninth century. Numerous traces of their iron mining and smelting in succeeding centuries have been found there. In the northern Transvaal the environment is quite similar to that of the neighboring Rhodesian plateau: moderately fertile, with rolling plains, light but adequate rainfall, and less harsh extremes of temperature.

Some parts of southern Africa are even richer in mineral deposits than the Rhodesian plateau, and these areas must have offered an incentive to settlement by the ancient Bantu ancestors. Various archeological sites show that iron, gold, tin, and copper were mined centuries before the arrival of settlers from Europe. In those areas where there were no mineral deposits, or where they were too difficult to exploit, there is evidence that the ancient peoples traded for metals from some distance.

In contrast with the Rhodesian plateau and Zambia, there has been disappointingly little archeological and historical research in South Africa and its neighbors. Even though there have been many

191

historians, anthropologists, and archeologists there during the twentieth century, their attention has been focused either on the study of the Bantu-speaking peoples today or on the exciting search for very ancient remains that illuminate the story of human evolution. The result is that science knows more of the Australopithecines and other ancestors of modern man than of Bantu history, and more of ancient Stone Age man than of the men of the Iron Age. The situation has been complicated by politics and racial prejudice; South Africa's European settlers have long pictured the Bantu-speaking peoples they conquered as inferior barbarians who arrived in the country at about the same time as the white man, and this has not encouraged efforts to reconstruct Bantu history.

For these reasons the earliest history of the Bantu settlement of South Africa and the surrounding countries must be sketched out in the most general terms, leaving many gaps. It is not until after about 1600, when both oral histories and written accounts begin to provide more concrete information, that southern Africa's history begins to appear as definitely and in as much detail as that farther north.

There is no evidence that the Bantu ancestors entered southern Africa, south of the Limpopo River, earlier than about A.D. 700–800. Before that time the entire region was populated by Stone Age peoples who spoke languages of the Khoisan stock: Khoi, Nama, Kung, Namib, Xam, and many others. These peoples, whom Europeans later came to call Bushmen and Hottentots, were the ancestral peoples of much of Africa south of the Sahara, and southern Africa was their last homeland after the

192

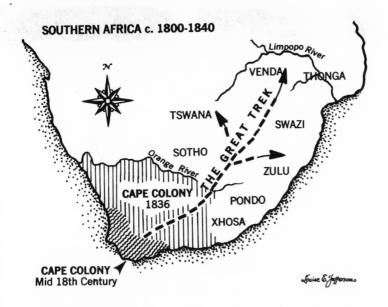

SOUTHERN AFRICA c. 1800-1840

Limpopo River

VENDA THONGA

TSWANA

THE GREAT TREK

SWAZI

SOTHO

Orange River

ZULU

CAPE COLONY
1836

PONDO

XHOSA

CAPE COLONY
Mid 18th Century

Louise E. Jefferson

Bantu and other African peoples from the north moved into their territories and absorbed or replaced them.

During the early period before the Bantu-speaking peoples arrived, the Khoisan peoples lived by hunting wild game and gathering wild foods. They were accomplished craftsmen in stone, but they were ignorant of pottery, ironwork, and agriculture. By the end of the first millennium some had apparently learned to herd domesticated animals, particularly sheep and goats, but they do not seem to have herded cattle until about the time the earliest ancestors of the Bantu arrived. Between about A.D. 1000 and 1600, however, cattle herding spread widely among those Khoisan peoples known as Hottentots. They were tending cattle as far south as the tip of the continent, around Cape Town, when the first Europeans settled that area in 1652.

The expansion of the Bantu-speaking peoples

into South Africa was undertaken from their settlements in the Zambia-Rhodesia-Mozambique territories, north of the Limpopo. The Gokomere peoples of that region are thought to have been the
group from which parties of settlers eventually
broke away to explore the lands south of the Limpopo. Pottery clearly related to that of the Gokomere potters has been found at Matokoma, a village
in the foothills of the Zoutpansberg Mountains in
the northern Transvaal. This pottery was made in
the ninth century, indicating that Gokomere offshoots had reached South Africa by that time, if
not a century or two earlier.

The next definite evidence of the Bantu expansion into South Africa comes from the discovery of
an iron-smelting furnace and scattered bits of pottery at Melville Koppies, not far from modern
Johannesburg in the central Transvaal. The pottery
there is different from that of the earlier Gokomere
type, but most archeologists believe it evolved
from Gokomere and thus was made by peoples
who were descended from or influenced by the
Gokomere peoples. The pottery found at Melville
Koppies is similar to that at another Transvaal site,
Uitkomst, and is part of the Uitkomst pottery tradition which has been found in many parts of the
Transvaal and neighboring Botswana.

At about the same time that the Uitkomst pottery was made at Melville Koppies, a rather different type was being made farther west, at a site
called Bambandyanalo, which is a village located
near the foot of Mapungubwe Hill. As the story of
Zimbabwe has already shown, that same area was
later heavily influenced by the royal culture which
194

built Zimbabwe, and it developed into a site of great wealth and prestige. But several centuries earlier Iron Age Bantu farmers had apparently settled around Mapungubwe, as a part of the general expansion to the south.

No definite dates have been revealed by archeology for the settling of other parts of South Africa. Yet when Vasco da Gama explored the Indian Ocean shores of South Africa, he made contact with Khoisan peoples in the far south and Negroid peoples, certainly early Bantu, all along the shores of what is today the province of Natal and the eastern Cape Province. There was no indication that they had only recently arrived in that area. It is certain, therefore, that the Bantu farmers and cattle herders were permanently in possession of the eastern Cape Province and the area farther north before about 1400; there is a real probability that they had gotten there by 1200 or 1300, although there were numerous smaller movements in and out of the area up until 1700.

The ancient period of the Bantu settlement of southern Africa can be summarized as follows.

Between A.D. 500 and 800 the first small parties of settlers moved into the northern Transvaal, and from that time until about 1200 they expanded to cover most of the Transvaal, northern Botswana, Swaziland, and Natal—moving ever farther south toward the Cape Province and the Orange Free State.

Between 1200 and 1450 the settlement of most of South Africa was complete, up to the lines that existed when the first Europeans made contact between 1500 and 1700. During this period other

195

Bantu ancestors had moved westward into the northern grasslands of Namibia, and were beginning to move slowly south into the increasingly arid lands around the Kalahari Desert.

The result of all this movement over a period of many centuries was the settlement of southern Africa by peoples of two large nations of Bantu speakers and several smaller ones. The largest were the Nguni group, spread along the Indian Ocean coast and inland in Swaziland, Natal, and Cape Province. Their main subdivisions were the Swazi, Zulu, and Xhosa. Next most numerous were the Sotho peoples, themselves subdivided into the Tswana group and the Sotho, and the latter were in turn grouped loosely into southern and northern branches. The Sotho covered parts of inland Natal, the Transvaal, the Orange Free State, Lesotho, and Botswana. Smaller groups were the Ovambo and Herero of Namibia, the Venda and Lemba of the Transvaal, and the Tonga of southern Mozambique.

Herero woman

All these peoples lived by a combination of farming and cattle raising, and most valued cattle very highly. In many areas the men spent their time tending the cattle. They cleared the lands for farming but left the actual cultivation to the women. The chief crops were sorghum and millet, beans, peanuts, and various vegetables. After the New World crop called maize (our corn) reached Africa during the sixteenth century, it was adopted by most of the southern Bantu as their principal staple, reducing sorghum and millet to subsidiary crops.

Much of southern Africa is either devoid of trees or sparsely covered by small trees. Wood was there-

196

fore a precious commodity in many areas, and was
rarely used in building except for frameworks
around which straw, dried mud, and cow dung
were plastered. Roofs of houses were usually made
of straw from the abundant tall grasses that grew
on the southern African plains. In much of the
Transvaal and Orange Free State, where trees were
very rare, stone was used to build both defensive
enclosures and houses. Numerous ruins of small
stone villages and houses dot the landscape in
these areas: An aerial archeological survey of thirty
square miles in the Orange Free State showed
about one site of stone ruins per square mile.

Venda man

From the evidence of oral histories it seems that
few of the southern Bantu peoples developed large,
centralized states before the seventeenth or eighteenth century. Before that time most were governed in relatively small chiefdoms, some of which
were grouped together into loose confederations
without a central governing body or king. The
failure of the southern Bantu-speaking peoples to
develop strong kingdoms and empires earlier in
their history was in no sense due to their being
more primitive than their kinsmen to the north, in
Kongo, Luba, Shona, and other nations. Rather,
it was because the land rarely supported dense
populations which could produce surplus food
or devote much time to mining, metalworking, or
other crafts. With their sparse populations scattered across large territories of plains and plateaus,
the southern Bantu found it unnecessary and im-
practical to form strong central governments. Their
resources were too precious to spend on supporting lavish courts, administrative structures, and

Ovambo woman

197

armies when these were not really necessary to ensure peace and a stable life. Only later, when changing conditions made it necessary, did they come together into kingdoms.

The rise of powerful kingdoms among the southern Bantu was in part due, ironically, to the encroachment of European settlers into the region. The European settlers, expanding northward and seeking vast plots of land for their cattle and grain, sealed off any possibility of further Bantu expansion to the south and eventually began to compete with the Bantu for grazing land. To understand this clearly, and to explore the dramatic developments that took place in southern Africa during the eighteenth and nineteenth centuries, it is necessary to digress for a moment.

Beaded sash, Matabele

The Portuguese were the first Europeans to explore the coastal lands of southern Africa, following Da Gama's expedition in 1498–99. They concentrated their settlements and trade stations near obvious sources of wealth, in Angola and Kongo in the west and Mozambique in the east, and paid South Africa scant attention. Occasionally Portuguese ships might anchor and send parties ashore for water or food, but since they found little evidence of trade in gold, ivory, or other precious commodities, their interest in South Africa was minimal.

When the Dutch began to compete with the Portuguese in the early seventeenth century, they eyed the rich Portuguese trade with the Far East hungrily. Dutch ships in large numbers began sailing into the Indian Ocean after 1600, and soon they were seizing Portuguese stations in India and In-

198

donesia, raiding Portuguese ships, and setting up competing trade arrangements. As their stake in the Far East grew, they found it necessary to establish way stations where their ships could rest, take on fresh supplies of water and food, and undertake repairs on the extremely long voyage between India and Holland. The tip of southern Africa, where an excellent natural harbor was to be found near Khoisan cattle country, was selected as the main Dutch base. In 1652 a party of Dutch soldiers and artisans landed at Table Bay to found Cape Town, on behalf of the Dutch East India Company. Led by Jan van Riebeeck, the mission had orders to build houses and warehouses and to organize the purchase of beef for Dutch ships from the Khoisan cattlemen.

The orders for Van Riebeeck's mission prohibited it from acquiring land or attempting any other activity which might interfere with the main object of procuring foodstuffs for the Company's ships. Very quickly, however, some of the party realized that there was profit to be made by raising

their own cattle and growing food for sale to the Company. By 1657 there were several independent Dutch burghers located a few miles from the Company's station, busily engaged in selling beef and grain for profit to the traders at Cape Town.

Very gradually more and more Dutchmen came to farm and raise cattle, and they slowly moved toward the interior and along the eastern coast in search of more land. As they moved they bought land from Khoisan chiefs when possible, or seized it by force. By 1702 the first parties of Dutch hunters had met and clashed with the Xhosa peoples, hundreds of miles to the east of Cape Town, thus beginning a process which was to bring tragedy to the Bantu-speaking peoples and a deep sickness into later South African society.

Life was harsh for the Dutch colonists and for later groups of French Huguenots who joined them. The soil they found was not very fertile, and the rainfall was fickle. Every few years the rains failed entirely, or fell in brief torrents for a short period and then failed for months. The Dutch East India Company's government on the Cape was stern, allowing the colonists the smallest measure of freedom and insisting on low, fixed prices for the beef, wild game, and wheat they brought in for sale. The colonists had frequent skirmishes and clashes with the Khoisan, who resented their imperious manners and their brutality. Many colonists who settled far into the interior made so little profit that they devoted themselves almost entirely to growing and hunting enough to feed themselves and their families, and they began to avoid contact with the government at Cape Town.

The general hardness of life for the Dutch colonists as they expanded away from Cape Town, combined with their resentment toward the Dutch East India Company, made them tough and hard-bitten. They came to regard the Khoisan "Hottentots" and other Africans as savages against whom the Dutch were pitted for survival in a harsh land. This attitude also brought a fierce, rugged sense of independence to the settlers; they were hostile to controls even by their own government. The average settler sought to move far away from the authority of Cape Town, where he could lay claim to thousands of acres of land; herd his cattle, sheep, and goats; hunt wild game; and become as self-sufficient as his talents and the land would allow. There were many similarities between the Dutch colonists and the British colonists of America, many of whom moved ever farther westward to escape the controls and restrictions of the better-established eastern seaboard, ruthlessly elbowing aside the native Indians whose lands they coveted.

The natural path for Dutch expansion was eastward, along the Indian Ocean coast. To the north and west of Cape Town the land becomes increasingly dry and infertile, while that to the east includes a narrow corridor of slightly higher rainfall. Even that corridor ends, not far from the modern port city of Port Elizabeth, in an arid area, although it resumes farther east, beyond East London, and becomes increasingly fertile along the coast of Natal.

Just as the most natural Dutch expansion was in an easterly direction, the earlier Bantu expansion had been westward from the Natal coast toward the southern Cape. The Xhosa peoples, who occupied that route, had stopped their migrations around 1600 in the area of the Fish River, west of which lay arid country. It was in that arid belt that the first contacts between the advance parties of Dutch colonists and the settled Xhosa cattlemen and grain farmers took place.

For several decades after the first clashes between the Dutch—who called themselves *Boers* ("farmers")—and the Xhosa there was tension between the two groups. During this period Boer hunters occasionally killed Xhosa cattle, and Xhosa warriors made raids to seize Boer cattle. Finally, in 1779, the Boer farmers organized a strong militia, and a full-scale war began. When it ended, after much devastation on both sides, the Boers had gained a victory and claimed several thousand acres of Xhosa land. This was the first in a series of wars between Boer and Xhosa which lasted a century, each followed by further Boer expansion into Xhosa territory.

The Boers had a clear military superiority over the Xhosa troops, although the latter had far more armed men. The Boers were excellent hunters, using their rifles with great accuracy, and they were skilled horsemen. Accustomed to a hard life of riding, shooting, hunting, and foraging for food,

202

they avoided pitched battles with the larger Xhosa forces and instead struck in lightning raids, killing warriors, burning villages, and destroying crops, livestock, and food supplies. The Xhosa were armed with spears, bows, and clubs. They owned no horses and had no experience with this brutal kind of war in which destruction of the crops and food stocks was a major tactic. Although they fought bravely and won many battles, they were inevitably forced to sue for peace as their people grew hungry and dispirited following repeated Boer cavalry raids.

As the Boer farmers increased in numbers and their needs for land grew, other parties began moving north from the Cape into the dry country called the Karroo. Although most of the Karroo was suitable only for herding small spreads of cattle on large ranches, the Boer thrusts eventually crossed it and reached the Orange River. On the north side of the Orange the rainfall becomes slightly higher, and range grasses grow more abundantly. Between 1760 and 1800 a small number of Boer families crossed the Orange and settled in the lands that today form the Orange Free State. There they met communities of Sotho peoples, and again clashes occurred. As in the wars with the Xhosa, however, the superior cavalry tactics of the Boers allowed them to press the Sotho slowly back, seizing portions of their land every few years.

The pressure of the Boers against the Xhosa on the Cape and the Sotho on the northern Cape and in the Orange Free State created a situation of overpopulation and political instability which was felt hundreds of miles to the north and east. Long before the Boers arrived, the African peoples had been in competition for the more favorable lands, and they had themselves gradually migrated west and south, into less desirable country, as their populations grew. The Boer advance not only sealed off any further possibility of expansion, but began to push back the African frontiers. Along the African-Boer frontiers, between 1750 and 1800, misery and uprooting of communities followed the Boer advance.

Zulu houses

Nearly five hundred miles northeast of the Boer-Xhosa frontier lies the heartland of the Zulu nation, located in one of the most fertile parts of the long corridor that stretches between the Drakensberg Mountains and the sea. From 1600 to 1750 population increased steadily in that prosperous country, and as it increased there was a gradual development of small states, ruled by chiefs, which protected their citizens from encroachment by surrounding states. As population density increased, so did the pressure for land and the political importance of the chiefs.

The peoples inhabiting this region were at the

time all members of the Nguni ethnic group but were divided into a number of smaller clans. Although these clans were closely related to each other in language and culture, their loyalties lay with their chiefdoms. By 1700, however, several chiefdoms had grown in power and influence, and had begun to expand by forcing the chiefs of neighboring states to swear fealty, to pay tribute, and to provide troops in time of war. The three most powerful of these expanded chiefdoms were the Ngwane, the Ndwandwe, and the Mthethwa. Their territories encompassed all of the lands that are today Swaziland, southern Mozambique, and northern Natal. Southward lay the lands of the Xhosa, covering southern Natal and the eastern Cape.

Competition for land had become an issue among the three northern Nguni federations even before the Boer-Xhosa wars began, but it became much more intense after the Boer advance sealed off the south and west from further expansion. In 1800 the three federations were ruled by strong leaders, who had expanded their influence over wide territories to create what were clearly beginning to resemble large kingdoms. At this date, however, the leaders were content to rule as paramount chiefs, allowing their subordinate chiefs to regard themselves as semi-sovereign vassals rather than as permanently conquered chiefs of provinces. The leaders of the three federated chiefdoms in 1800 were Chief Sobhuza of the Ngwane, Chief Zwide of the Ndwandwe, and Chief Dingiswayo of the Mthethwa.

Warfare among the three federations, at this

time in their history, consisted largely of cattle raids and forays by warriors to seize grain. The warriors were loosely organized by ethnic group, every contingent being under the command of its chief or subchief. Their weapons were spears and large, stout shields of cowhide. In a typical battle two forces would advance against each other, hurl their long spears, then fall back. If one party suffered greater casualties than the other, it retreated from the field of battle, while the victorious troops seized whatever cattle and grains they could find in the area, then withdrew to their own territory. Battles were fought during the day, with both parties retiring to their camps at night. Wars were short, usually lasting no more than a few days. Following a war the troops returned to their villages, where they resumed their duties as cattlemen and farmers.

In 1787 a young son was born to the chief of the Zulu clan, which was at the time one of a number of subordinate chiefdoms within the Mthethwa federation. His name was Shaka, and he was to become one of the greatest figures in African history. Like Caesar, Genghis Khan, and Alexander the Great, he was destined to build a military empire that would have cataclysmic effects over a vast territory.

Shaka was only one of many sons of the Zulu chief, and legend tells that he was born out of wedlock. Under ordinary circumstances he would have lived an inconspicuous life and been quickly forgotten by later generations. Shaka was, however, no ordinary man, and he was born in a time of ferment and opportunity. As he grew into young

Shaka

manhood he proved to have enormous physical strength and courage—he was able to best his adversaries in combat with little effort. By the time he was twenty he was known as the fiercest warrior in the Zulu army, and over the next few years he distinguished himself in a number of wars in which the Zulus fought under Dingiswayo's banner.

When Shaka was about twenty-five his father died, and Dingiswayo used his influence to have

Shaka proclaimed head of the Zulu chiefdom, in appreciation of his outstanding service in the Mthethwa army. Over the next few years Shaka began to use his brilliant military talents and his genius as a leader of men to build the Zulu chiefdom into a new kind of state, with a reorganized and greatly strengthened army as its core.

Shaka's first moves were in the military arena. Before he became chief the Zulu, like other Nguni peoples, had organized their society on the basis of male age grades. Each boy was considered part of a formal age grade, and throughout his life his status and friendships were defined by the age group to which he belonged. As each age grade grew older, its members were raised to new levels of prestige in society. Shaka took the age-grade system and made it the basis of Zulu militarism by declaring that all men in certain age grades, from the late teens to middle age, were automatically part of the army unless physically unfit for service. Members of each age grade were considered regiments in the Zulu army and were given their own banners, their own leaders, and their own sense of unity.

At the same time Shaka prohibited the use of the traditional long-handled spear of the Nguni and instead required that each man march into battle carrying a spear with a short, thick handle and a long blade. The short spear, called an *assegai,* was used for stabbing and slashing in hand-to-hand combat. Its long, sharp blade was almost as effective as that of a broadsword. Each man was protected by a great cowhide shield, from five to six feet long and up to three feet wide. Any

Warrior with assegai

soldier who returned from battle without his *assegai* was severely punished, usually by death.

The Zulu army was put through increasingly rigorous training, and soon Shaka introduced new battle formations. The most frequently used, and the best, was the "cow horn" formation. In its center were several ranks of men, marching shoulder to shoulder, protected by their stout shields. On each end was a contingent of warriors trained to advance in quickstep, so that the ends of the formation could rapidly curve to attack a besieged enemy's flanks or swing around to rush into the enemy's rear guard while its main force was engaged with the center of the Zulu line.

Most of these innovations were introduced between 1815 and 1818, and during that period the Zulu regiments became the strongest in the Mthethwa army. In 1815 or 1816 the two other large Nguni federated chiefdoms, the Ngwane and the Ndwandwe, went to war against each other. The Ndwandwe, under the leadership of Chief Zwide, routed the Ngwane army in a series of battles. Finally, after crushing defeats, the Ngwane nation, led by Chief Sobhuza, migrated northward into what is today Swaziland and there established themselves permanently as the Swazi nation. Even though defeated by the Ndwandwe, the Ngwane were a proud, internally united nation, and they had great respect for their talented leader, Sobhuza. In their new homeland they soon developed a well-organized state, with Sobhuza as its king. One of his descendants, Sobhuza, is the king and political leader of the modern nation of Swaziland.

Having forced the Ngwane to migrate, the

powerful Ndwandwe turned their eyes toward Dingiswayo's Mthethwa chiefdom. In 1818 the armies of the two federations met in a great battle, which resulted in a complete rout of the Mthethwa and the death of Dingiswayo. For some reason which oral histories do not make clear, Shaka's Zulu army was not present at the battle. Had it taken part in the fighting, the outcome might have been different. As it developed, however, the Mthethwa were completely disorganized, and Shaka's powerful army emerged as the only capable fighting force in the federation.

Shaka seized the opportunity quickly and proclaimed himself king of a new state, in which the Zulus were the central people. Various tribes of Mthethwa were brought under the Zulu system, and Shaka decreed that they would from that time forward be Zulus, like his own people.

Almost immediately the Ndwandwe, greatly superior in numbers and flushed with their recent successes against Sobhuza and Dingiswayo, marched their victorious army against Shaka. In an epic battle Shaka's small but magnificently disciplined troops put up a brilliant defense against great odds and held the Ndwandwe at bay until they retired. A few days later, with both armies rested and eager for battle, they came together again, and this time Shaka's army took the offensive in one of the greatest battles in African history. Relentlessly it drove into the massive ranks of Ndwandwe soldiers, marching in tight formation with grim faces and shouts of anger. The Ndwandwe began to falter, and soon, after several hours of fighting, their army was split into several pieces

210

and they began to flee in a total rout. In a glittering display of valor and discipline, the small Zulu army stood alone on the battlefield, having rendered a decisive defeat to an army that outnumbered it nearly three to one.

The Ndwandwe federation itself was shattered by this defeat, and two of its most powerful chiefs led their nations on long migrations out of harm's way. One group, under Soshangane, moved into southern Mozambique, where it organized the empire of Gaza. The other, under Zwangendaba, marched onto the Rhodesian plateau and delivered the coup de grâce to the decaying empire of Changamire, sacking the great temples at Zimbabwe in the process. Zwide, formerly the paramount chief of a large Nguni federation, was left with a shrunken territory and a severely diminished force of warriors.

Shaka was a great leader who had a deep intuitive sense of when and how to seize opportunity. Following the defeat of Zwide's Ndwandwe, he gathered together as many of the fragments of the federation as he could and incorporated their people into his Zulu nation. Subchiefs who refused to accept this merger were summarily executed, or fled to escape Shaka's vengeance. But their ordinary followers, and their women, children, and herds were placed immediately under Zulu authority, and they rapidly lost any identity except that of being Zulu. Within a few years Shaka had trebled or quadrupled the population of his Zulu nation, and he maintained the entire nation on a military footing.

Around his own court Shaka built vast barracks,

in which he housed thousands of his soldiers. Food-stuffs flowed in from his subjects and from conquered peoples to feed this huge and expanding military center. The men were given rigorous training and physical-fitness exercises. Each day they ran, wrestled with each other, and practiced double-time marches in tight formation. They had daily practice in hand-to-hand combat and were lectured on the stern military virtues which Shaka proclaimed to be necessary for all Zulus. Laziness, cowardice, and disobedience were severely punished, while accomplishments were honored and praised.

Shaka's proud army spent only a part of its time in its barracks undergoing this training. Frequently units were sent on campaigns to extend the kingdom's territory and to annex new tribes. Wars were declared against various neighbors, and in each the Zulu army was victorious. Within a few years Shaka had built an empire which covered much of the modern province of Natal, and his influence was respected and feared far beyond his borders.

The threat of Zulu militarism forced surrounding peoples either to migrate to safer countries or to form themselves into kingdoms which could offer some defense. Many of those who migrated adopted Zulu military tactics, and they in turn scourged the lands through which they marched seeking new homes. Like Zwangendaba and Soshangane, another Nguni chieftain named Mzilikazi led his people on a long march of conquest northward. Acquiring the name Ndebele (or Matabele) en route, they made their way through the Transvaal, but were constantly harassed by various Sotho groups already established there and by Boer settlers who had entered the area. Eventually Mzilikazi's people settled in the western portion of the Rhodesian plateau, displacing the Shona peoples there, and established Matabeleland, a new kingdom of Nguni peoples far from their original home.

The Zulu expansion had its greatest effects to the west, in the region around the Drakensberg Mountains and the high plateau west of the mountains. There many groups of the Sotho nation had long been settled. On various occasions Zulu armies marched against them, but Zulu campaigns against neighboring Nguni groups sent these groups, in turn, on campaigns of conquest and pillage among the peaceful Sotho. Out of this upheaval emerged the kingdom of Basutoland in the 1820's.

Like the Nguni, the Sotho were previously not organized into strong, centralized kingdoms, but lived instead in a series of small chiefdoms. Before the rise of the Zulu military threat, they had found it unnecessary to come together into formal states. During Shaka's aggressive expansion, however, many of the Sotho communities were raided and sent in flight from the powerful Zulu armies, and it became essential, for self-protection if for no other reason, for them to develop greater unity.

The drive for Sotho unity was led by a young chief named Moshesh, chief of a small Sotho group, who brought his people together for mutual protection around the Drakensberg Mountains. After seeking strong defensive sites for several years, Moshesh settled his people, in 1824, around a series of hills at Thaba Bosiu. There they were able to

213

Moshesh

stand off every army that marched against them,
partly by stout military defenses and partly by
Moshesh's astute diplomacy. Moshesh was deeply
committed to peace, although he was willing to
do battle when necessary, and he became one of
the most effective statesmen in southern African
history. He welcomed various shattered Sotho peoples into his kingdom, accomplishing the building
of a united nation by gentleness much as Shaka
was doing at the same time by force. Moshesh
volunteered to pay occasional tribute in cattle to
Shaka, thus protecting his kingdom from a full-
scale onslaught of Zulu military might. Year by
year his kingdom grew, and with it the strength
to withstand attacks when Moshesh's statesmanship failed.

Unlike Shaka, Moshesh recognized that Africans
must learn European military tactics and techniques if they were to protect themselves in the
future. He collected reports on the actions of Boer
pioneers and hunters who were moving in the direction of his kingdom, and he sent emissaries into
the Cape to buy arms, ammunition, and horses.

214

During the 1830's his Basuto nation developed an army unit which was mounted on horseback and which possessed guns the men were skilled in using. Moshesh never used this military strength for expanding his kingdom, but he continued to add to his defensive capability. When his kingdom later came under attack from Boer commandos, he was one of the few African leaders who was able to meet them on more or less equal terms with mounted, armed troops.

Basuto man

In Zululand itself Shaka used the years following his assumption of power to strengthen the government and bind the nation together into an effective kingdom. In this effort he was brilliantly successful. Within ten years the Zulu nation had vastly expanded in both area and population, and its people had developed enormous pride in their nation. Many, however, eventually wearied of the incessant bloody military campaigns and the vengeful sternness with which Shaka ruled his kingdom. In 1828, when his power was at its peak, Shaka was assassinated by his brother Dingane, who became the second king of the Zulu nation. Shaka's reign lasted only ten years, but within that brief period he completely revolutionized both the Nguni peoples and the affairs of much of South Africa. At his death the Zulu were the most powerful and well organized people in southern Africa.

As these momentous events were taking place among the Zulu and Sotho peoples, another fateful force was building on the Cape. In 1795, during the Napoleonic War, Britain occupied Cape Town; it handed it back to Holland in 1803, then reoccupied it permanently in 1806. With British rule

215

there developed a new set of policies in the Cape region, including the extension of the government's authority far into the interior, into the lands of the independent Boer farmers. British rule also brought the question of slavery into the foreground, since Britain was itself in the process of abolishing the slave trade and using its influence to end slavery wherever possible. The Boers had long owned African slaves, and had developed a haughty and contemptuous attitude toward Africans in general. In 1836, disgusted by the effects of British policy, large numbers of Boers began to leave the Cape entirely, marching north with their families and herds on the Great Trek, looking for new lands where they would be free of British interference.

The Great Trek took large, well-armed parties of Boer pioneers into the Orange Free State, the Transvaal, and Natal. In a great battle with Mzilikazi's Ndebele, who were temporarily settled in the southern Transvaal, the Boers won a victory which gave them possession of a large part of that region and forced the Ndebele to resume their

216

march into Rhodesia. In the Orange Free State the Boers came into frequent conflict with Moshesh's Basuto nation, whose cavalry were tougher adversaries than most other Africans the Boers had faced. Although the Boers were unable to inflict a decisive defeat on the Basuto troops, they gradually occupied portions of Moshesh's lands, including the more fertile region. Finally, in 1868, Moshesh negotiated a treaty with Britain by which he placed his kingdom under the protection of the British crown, thus saving what was left of his lands from further Boer encroachment.

One arm of the Great Trek marched from the Orange Free State eastward, through the Drakensbergs, into Zululand and Natal. Between 1836 and 1838 several fierce battles erupted between the Boers and Dingane's Zulus, and for the first time the Zulus found a foe too strong for them. Boer guns cut down thousands of Zulus, as they marched against the Boer lines in tight formation, and Dingane was forced to concede to the Boers a large portion of his territory in 1838. His prestige greatly weakened by this humiliating defeat, Dingane was deposed in 1840 by his brother Mpande, who adopted a policy of negotiation and conciliation toward both the Boers and the British. British settlers were beginning by this time to settle along Natal's coast, and there were frequent conflicts between the two European groups between 1840 and 1880. In 1878 Mpande's successor, Cetewayo, became involved in the struggle between Boer and Briton, and in 1879 his army was crushed by a powerful British force. The result was that the Zulu nation came under British control; even

217

though the authority of its kings was recognized, the Zulu nation was no longer sovereign after this time, and ultimately became a part of the Union of South Africa.

Boer advances far to the west, along the borders of modern Botswana, resulted in a tragic series of conflicts between the Boer commandos and the peaceful Tswana people, who had never developed a military tradition. Their chiefs, powerless to offer any effective resistance to Boer attacks, welcomed British missionaries and trading agents, and sought British protection against the Boers. The British presence served to stave off Boer seizure of Tswana territory, and in 1885 the Tswana chiefdoms were formally placed under the protection of the British crown, as the protectorate of Bechuanaland.

The same process was repeated far to the north, in the lands of the Swazi, where Sobhuza had built a small but tightly knit kingdom following his flight from Dingiswayo. Swaziland's isolation from the centers of Boer and British settlements rendered it safe long after both the Tswana and the Sotho began to suffer from European expansion. In the 1890's, however, it was briefly annexed by the South African Republic in the Transvaal, which hoped to use it as a corridor to the sea. Britain forced the Transvaal to repeal the annexation, however, and almost immediately placed Swaziland under British protection.

The Xhosa, who were the first of the Bantu-speaking peoples to come face to face with the aggressive power of the expanding Boers, maintained their independence, despite repeated defeats, over a full century of wars. By 1880, however,

218

they were almost completely surrounded by European settlers and governments, and were forced to accept incorporation into the British Cape Territory.

The nineteenth century proved to be the era of the most glorious achievements of the southern Bantu-speaking peoples, and at the same time their period of greatest tragedy. In little more than half a century they had produced Shaka and his brilliant, terrible Zulu empire, with its formidable military and political might. In the same period gentle Moshesh, with statesmanship, vision, and great courage, created the kingdom of Basutoland out of chaos. Sobhuza built his small nation into a proud kingdom in the green hills of Swaziland. But the relentless advance of European settlers and colonial ambitions took a sad toll in lives and in human dignity, as Xhosa, Tswana, Sotho, and other peoples valiantly fought a losing battle against overwhelming odds.

As the century ended, the Basuto, Tswana, and Swazi were safe from total submersion under the tide of European conquest, but their Bantu relatives had lost the long battle and had been forced to accept incorporation into a white-ruled South Africa. Today their plight is one of the world's gravest problems. Their past accomplishments have been ground into the dust of white rule, and they live as a subject population, in virtual slavery.

Sobhuza II, present-day king of Swaziland

9

The Fate of
the Bantu Achievement

The expansion of the Bantu civilization throughout Africa south of the equator, and the gradual creation of great states and empires, represents a triumph in the face of considerable odds. Yet between 1700 and 1900 many of the most notable creations of the Bantu-speaking peoples suffered a poignant decline, especially when faced with the growing influence of Western ideas and power. What were the hallmarks of the Bantu civilization, and what were the weaknesses that caused it to erode so quickly when challenged from the outside world?

The Bantu achievement was most marked in six areas of life: agriculture, metal technology, crafts, architecture, politics, and creative ideas in

220

religion, philosophy, and oral literature. At first glance, the Bantu contributions in these areas seem commonplace when compared with those of such ancient Mediterranean peoples as the Egyptians, Sumerians, Greeks, and Romans. Yet when seen in the perspective of a vast, isolated, inhospitable environment, very insulated from the rest of the world, they reflect a great strength of adaptability and creativity.

In agriculture the Bantu achievement was the ability to adapt a basic knowledge of plants, land cultivation, and soil conservation to a wide variety of soil and climate conditions—almost all of which were somewhat less than generous. The very earliest ancestors of the Bantu-speaking peoples who spread out from the Katanga cradleland were tenacious farmers. They knew how to acquire supplemental foods from fishing, hunting wild game, and gathering a large variety of wild fruits, berries, roots, nuts, and seeds. But they concentrated their efforts on clearing the land of trees and underbrush in order to plant their crops of millet, sorghum, peas, beans, and many kinds of leafy vegetables.

The soil in which the Bantu farmers planted their crops had to be prepared and tended with great skill and care. It was mostly covered with tough grasses, thick wild shrubs, and trees with very hard wood. Under this natural plant cover the fertile layer was thin and relatively poor in the humus and nutrients needed to produce a good yield. One or two years of planting tended to deplete this scant natural fertility. Years of rest were necessary so that the native weeds, grasses, and shrubs could reestablish themselves, deposit

221

leaves and twigs which decomposed to introduce new nutrients into the topsoil, and restore a measure of fertility. In most areas the rainfall was light and unreliable. For a few months of each year rain fell, sometimes in heavy downpours, and the rest of the year was dry.

Adding further perils to agriculture were the many insects which destroyed crops and the plant diseases which ruined those crops that had not developed an immunity to them. The tropical warmth of the climate and the unevenness of the rainfall combined, ironically, to create further difficulties in maintaining healthy crops. Fallen leaves, weeds, twigs, and branches decompose, in every part of the world, then gradually sink into the soil to deposit chemical nutrients as bacteria continue to decompose them. In most of tropical Africa the decomposition process is speeded up by the constant warmth, so that the natural nutrients form on or very near the surface of the soil. Heavy rains tend to wash away some of these nutrients before they mix thoroughly with the soil. Through the process known as leaching, more of these essential nutrients are also washed downward too rapidly through the topsoil, finally becoming deposited at a deeper level than is normally cultivated. Between the leaching and the washing away, it is very difficult for the soil of tropical Africa to build up and retain a reasonable degree of fertility.

The skills of the Bantu farmer gradually developed a pattern which was the best under the circumstances: the shifting plot system. When the farmers slashed down the trees and undergrowth covering a plot, they burned them so that the ashes

222

would add useful chemical elements to the soil.
After planting and harvesting one or two crops,
they would either rotate less demanding crops
for another year or two or move on to another
plot. The original plot would be left to nature for
regeneration. This system requires large acreages
for each family and appears to be a wasteful use
of land. Yet it is the only method which works in
most African soils, until there is available the money
and knowledge to add artificial fertilizers and to
grow certain kinds of cover crops which replenish
the soil's fertility more rapidly than nature can do.
This advanced kind of knowledge was not available
to the Bantu farmers; it is a relatively new thing
even in scientific Western agriculture.

In some areas the Bantu civilization went beyond
its basic system of agriculture, when local opportunities offered. In parts of Rhodesia, Tanzania,
and Mozambique lands were terraced to prevent
the erosion of soil and to retain as much of the
rainfall as possible. In the Interlacustrine Region
and some of the neighboring highlands cattle dung
was used to fertilize the crops, enriching the soil
greatly.

Seen from the perspective of history and a knowledge of the problems posed by the African environment, the Bantu civilization's agricultural accomplishments were impressive. Theirs was no land
flowing with milk and honey, but the Bantu-speaking peoples used their knowledge of plants and the
soil creatively and flexibly to earn the best living
possible. Where local areas were better watered
and more fertile, they developed the best ways of
producing abundant yields. Where lands were more

arid and less fertile, they grew crops as best they could, then grazed herds of cattle, sheep, and goats to provide an alternate source of food. When necessary they fished and hunted. Although the pattern of making a living varied according to the bountifulness of the land they settled, they made the best possible use of it to expand their population and live as comfortably as they could.

The ability to use metals was the second hallmark of the Bantu civilization. Scholars disagree on whether the knowledge of mining, smelting, and forging iron was independently discovered in Africa or was brought there from the Middle East, where it was known as early as 1500 B.C. Whatever the origin of this knowledge, however, Africans throughout the continent used it to great advantage. The Bantu-speaking peoples used it, at least as early as the time of Christ, to make axes, hoes, adzes, knives, needles, scissors, and many other tools. If they had not been able to make these iron tools, they could never have spread their agricultural way of life across central and southern Africa. Stone tools, however useful they may have been to more primitive hunting peoples, were not adequate to the tasks of clearing large fields of stout trees and shrubs, and cultivating the harsh soil. The Bantu civilization was built almost as much on its mastery of iron as on its knowledge of agriculture. In every new area the men who understood metallurgy quickly located available iron deposits. They dug out the ore, built highly effective small furnaces, and smelted out the crude iron from the ore. With simple but efficient forges and bellows they were able to melt the iron, then fashion it into the tools they needed. Where iron was more plentiful it was used for weapons as well as tools, although tools were considered more important when the supplies of iron were scarce.

The basic skill in metallurgy was used, of course, not only for iron but for copper, tin, and gold, if they were available. However, they were rarely considered to be of the same value as iron. Generally they were used to make ornaments and art objects, or, when the opportunity existed, to trade to the outside world for especially valuable goods.

Today the countries of Zaire, Zambia, Rhodesia, and South Africa are the richest mineral-producing countries in Africa, as they were in ancient times long before the Europeans came. Literally hundreds of thousands of ancient mines have been found within their territories. It was the lure of gold, silver, and copper that aroused Portugal's interest in Angola and Kongo. The gold and iron that were exported from the Rhodesian plateau down to the sea at Sofala were the mainstays of the great Swahili trading cities, as well as the magnets that drew the Portuguese up the Zambezi into the lands of Mwene Mutapa.

*Present-day
African miner*

In working all these metals the Bantu-speaking peoples showed a mastery of all phases of basic metallurgy. There were few deposits, other than those deep under the earth's surface, that escaped the keen eyes of their artisans and miners. Their metal tools were well shaped, with hard, sharp blades and points. When working copper and gold the Bantu craftsmen developed devices for making fine wire and paper-thin plate, as well as gold tacks and nails which were used to secure gold wire and foil to wooden statues. Handsome cups and bowls were hammered to exquisite smoothness for the use of the nobility. Attractive beads, bangles, bracelets, necklaces, and belts were fashioned in iron, copper, and gold to adorn the wealthy and the noble.

Mangbetu jug

Most of the Bantu-speaking peoples achieved a notable level of crafts: pottery, musical instruments, woven baskets, stools, gongs, cloth of cotton and bark, and intricately carved staffs and maces for men of position. Utilitarian objects for the common people were simple but attractive, and were carefully designed and made to serve useful functions. For cooking and eating there were many sizes and shapes of pots, bowls, and pitchers made of clay. In areas where trees were plentiful, bowls for serving and eating were often finely carved in hard woods. Where soft stone was available, it was frequently used to make similar vessels, some of which were elegant in their clean lines and superb craftsmanship. Spoons and forks were made from wood, stone, or bone in great variety. Needles, scissors, and shears were generally made from iron. Well-made, attractive combs and hair ornaments were

226

fashioned of bone, shell, wood, or metal, depending on what materials were available.

For the nobility and the wealthy, considerable artistry was used in both ornamental and utilitarian objects. Pottery vessels with very thin but strong walls were made in graceful shapes and decorated with lovely designs. Often they were carefully burnished and colored. Masks and statues for religious and ceremonial purposes were intricately made, and were passed down from generation to generation as objects of veneration. Eating utensils and bowls were sometimes made from gold or copper—materials much too precious to be owned by the commoner.

Little is known of the ancient crafts of weaving and spinning, although spindle whorls of clay, stone, and metal have been found in many graves and at the ruins of many towns. Animal skins, crude wool, cotton, coconut fiber, raffia, and bark were all used for making clothing. Again the clothing of the nobility was richer than that of commoners. In several Bantu kingdoms threads of gold were spun into royal robes, and clips and fasteners of gold and copper were often used for the robes of the highborn.

Even though most Bantu-speaking peoples have left no great ruined temples and buildings as magnificent as those of Egypt, Greece, and Mesopotamia, their techniques of construction were meritorious. In most parts of their territory they found little stone useful for building purposes. Generally the only easily available material was earth, which, mixed with water and straw, hardened into a very suitable covering for houses. Houses built of this

material were constructed around a wooden framework, and roofs were made of thatch from the tall grasses that grow on most of the African savannas.

The houses were simple but comfortable. They were able to withstand many years of the typical weather conditions of central and southern Africa. And since the agricultural rotation pattern required that villages move every few years, few of the Bantu peoples found it worthwhile to build houses that would last longer than necessary. The houses were often decorated with geometric designs, frequently painted or etched with colors made of mineral ores and naturally occurring chemicals.

In some moister areas, such as the Interlacustrine Region, the extremely tall grasses of the area were used as a prime building material. In Buganda, for example, grasses and reeds were commonly used to produce truly elegant houses. The houses of the noble and wealthy people were very large, often with rooms more than thirty feet across, and were

light and airy because of the material used. In these areas the weaving of reeds and grasses was developed to heights of real artistry. In the houses of royalty among the Baganda and the Kuba, grasses were woven into intricate abstract designs. The first European visitors to see these houses were struck by their beauty. Even today, when few African craftsmen practice these ancient arts, tourists are quick to photograph the woven houses they find—not because of their novelty but because of the extraordinary grace and beauty with which they are made.

In those areas where stone was readily available, such as the Rhodesian plateau and the northern parts of South Africa, the craftsmen of the Bantu civilization turned their talents to working in that durable material. Eventually they were able to build the hundreds of temples, enclosures, and other structures that dot that region today, and are so impressively symbolized by the brooding ruins at Great Zimbabwe.

Apart from these great stone ruins, of course, no one will argue that the Bantu civilization has left the world an outstanding architectural legacy. But the construction of houses and the plans of villages and towns were functional and intelligently designed. Towns were laid out with care to take advantage of natural drainage and the contours of the land. In areas where defense was a problem they were surrounded by trenches or thick walls to keep enemies at bay. The streets were often broad and straight, and were bordered by fences. Neatness and cleanliness were considered important. For a people who moved often, and whose lands produced little surplus wealth, the Bantu craftsmen performed well.

Another hallmark of the Bantu civilization, which can be appreciated only by what one finds today, was its achievement in the intellectual and esthetic field. Apart from the Swahili, no Bantu people developed a system of writing prior to the arrival of the Europeans; hence we have no written record of their ancient poetry, philosophy, religion, myths, and folktales. From what has been learned since the European contact, however, it is apparent that their accomplishments in this area were worthy ones.

Every Bantu society produces bards who specialize in memorizing and retelling its accumulated lore and wisdom. The best of these bards can speak eloquently for days on the lives and exploits of their great kings. These oral histories have produced epic literatures that can be thrilling in their dramatic presentation. Each serves to preserve the morals and virtues of the society, so the storyteller may spend hours describing the qualities of the great kings of the past: their piety, their bravery, their wisdom, their generosity, their charity to the unfortunate, their mercy toward enemies, and their great concern for the welfare of their people.

In some Bantu societies, such as those of Burundi and Rwanda, the aristocracy for many generations has devoted itself to the development of poetry and oral literature. A gifted Rwandan poet can recite for hours graceful epic poems which he has composed over a period of years, constantly refining and perfecting them.

Every Bantu society has produced its sages, who

are looked to for the clearest statements of that society's religious and philosophical beliefs. The sages of Kongo, for example, reveal systems of belief about God, man, and the world which are extremely complex and elaborate, and which are sometimes beautiful in conception. In great detail they tell about God and how and why He created man. They tell of God's purpose in creating the seasons, the sky, the mountains, rivers, waterfalls, and other things on earth. Every natural phenomenon is given an explanation: the stars, the moon, the sun, the tides, the movements of heavenly bodies.

Just as al-Masudi was impressed, in the tenth century, by the Bantu orators he found on his visit to the Swahili coast, almost everyone who knows Bantu culture today is struck by the eloquence of its great speakers. The man who can speak gracefully and with dramatic expression is honored, and people praise him for his retelling of a national epic or his delivery of a good rhyme, a clever riddle, a popular fable, or a telling parable.

Children's stories are told around the fires at dusk, usually by grandfathers or grandmothers who have special talent for entertaining and educating the young. The best of these older storytellers are never at a loss for a good tale that may send the children into peals of laughter or shivers of fear. Sometimes their stories contain moral messages, but some are purely for entertainment.

Of all the qualities of the Bantu civilization, the most vivid is that of its politics and government. The many kinds of government that the Bantu created during the two-thousand-year period of

231

their settlement of southern Africa were elaborate and effective. They maintained internal peace and tranquillity, at their best, as well as any governments in any part of the world. They produced leaders of enormous vision and political talent: Affonso, Changamire, Shaka, and Moshesh, to name only a few.

The systems of government which the Bantu civilization evolved differed, of course, from region to region and group to group. But they typically were organized around a king who was believed to rule with divine approval, and often to possess semidivine powers himself. His powers were great, and he had authority over almost all the affairs of his kingdom. Yet there were safeguards against unjust actions by the king. He had powerful ministers and advisers around him, whose opinions counted when decisions were made. He ruled over a land in which local chiefs, heads of families, and councils of elders also had power. If he ruled harshly and unwisely, there were factions which might depose him, and this happened from time to time in the history of every Bantu kingdom. When he grew old or ill, he was expected to abdicate his throne so that a younger, more able king could provide the leadership.

The Bantu system of government could not, of course, prevent occasional despotism; no system of government ever devised by man has been totally successful in guaranteeing that its rulers would be wise and just. But the Bantu peoples resented injustice and harsh rule as much as any people. When they found themselves ruled by a man whom they regarded as unfit, they could and did act. Even

232

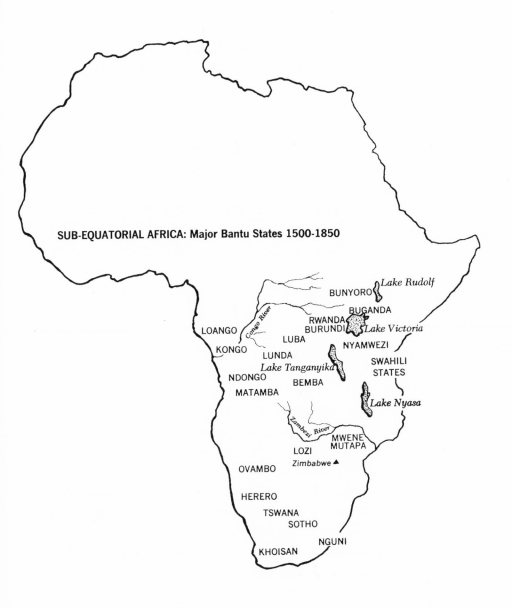

SUB-EQUATORIAL AFRICA: Major Bantu States 1500-1850

Lake Rudolf

BUNYORO

BUGANDA

RWANDA
BURUNDI *Lake Victoria*

LOANGO

Congo River

KONGO

LUBA

NYAMWEZI

LUNDA

Lake Tanganyika

SWAHILI
STATES

NDONGO

BEMBA

MATAMBA

Lake Nyasa

Zambezi River

MWENE
MUTAPA

LOZI

OVAMBO

Zimbabwe ▲

HERERO

TSWANA

SOTHO

NGUNI

KHOISAN

the great Shaka, one of the most powerful and forceful kings ever to rise to power within the Bantu civilization, was assassinated by his brother and a faction of notables who resented his obsessive military campaigns and expenditures.

In all the governments of the Bantu people there was a measure of democracy, although it was a very different kind of democracy from that of modern Europe and America. There were rarely formal political parties and systematic votes. In each village and district, however, the affairs of the state were studied and discussed daily by the elders and the men of local power. They sent their views to the provincial rulers and the king's cabinet, so that the king could act in full knowledge of the views of his subjects. While Europe was still in the Dark Ages, and millions of serfs lived out their lives with no power to influence their rulers, there were Bantu states where peasants had opinions about government, and ways to register those opinions. A wise king listened to their views, while an unwise king disregarded them, sometimes to his own peril.

In all these areas the Bantu civilization distinguished itself in the face of handicaps and difficulties. If one compares the Bantu civilization with those of Greece, Rome, western Europe, Egypt, India, and China, however, it seems at first glance to be a modest one. Its technology was effective, but it never reached the impressive heights scaled by these civilizations. In its oral literature, philosophy, and arts it may have been gifted and creative, but they were never recorded in writing or carried to the elaborate lengths found in these other civilizations. In the face of such

234

comparisons, must we judge the Bantu achievement to be of a lesser order?

Any civilization must be judged in terms of how
well its people are able to seize the opportunities
afforded by their environment. The Bantu-speaking
peoples were faced with two environmental difficulties which set unsurmountable limits; yet they
were able to achieve much in spite of these
difficulties.

First, and very importantly, the lands of central
and southern Africa have long been meager in their
fertility, especially when compared with the enor-
mously rich valleys of the Nile, the Indus, the
Tigris, and the Euphrates. Not until the development of modern agricultural science has there been
any possibility of wresting better yields from the
soil than the Bantu farmers were able to produce.
Even today Western-trained agricultural scientists
and engineers are facing an uphill battle in the
Bantu lands.

Second, the Bantu civilization was almost totally
isolated from the great currents of thought and
development which swept the countries around
the Mediterranean and enabled the peoples of Europe to rise from barbarism. Except for those who
lived in the narrow strip of land along the Indian
Ocean, no members of the Bantu society had any
opportunity to interact with different peoples, to
learn new ways of solving problems, or to develop
new methods of making a living. Throughout the
history of mankind isolation has been a handicap,
especially in the fields of technology and industry.
When one considers that virtually everything the
Bantu civilization accomplished was from the ef-

forts of its own people, without benefit of new ideas and challenges from the rest of the world, it again begins to appear impressive.

In the realms of life where individual talent seems to make the most difference, the comparison between the Bantu civilization and others shows less inequality. The music, dance, and art of the Bantu peoples are of high esthetic quality by any standard. Artists from Europe and Asia today feel awe and deep appreciation when they view the sculpture or hear the music of Bantu Africa. They recognize that the men and women who produced African art were inspired by the same deep feelings that move all great artists, and that they expressed those inspirations for the appreciation of all men.

In their social and political life, too, the Bantu people developed concepts and practices that command the respect of all. Their ideas of justice, of good and evil, of order among peoples, and of wise leadership were mature and intelligent. They

236

knew what human misery and degradation were, and they developed ideas and systems of government which helped, as much as any system could, to give each person a sense of dignity and worth. One of the great ironies of history was that the Bantu peoples often pitied or despised the Europeans who conquered them, because they felt that the Europeans had been unable to learn the great concepts of civilized behavior that the Bantu way of life regarded as natural.

For all this, however, there was a weakness in the Bantu civilization which is best described as fragility. This quality grew out of the poverty of the land, and it made the Bantu civilization vulnerable to conquest and imposed change, once a stronger, more determined military and political force faced it from the outside world. Basically, this fragility was a simple thing: One man, by his hardest effort, could support only his family, with very little food or goods left over. He had little leisure time to speculate about new and better ways of doing things. There were few surplus resources to support an elaborate court, a large army, a great class of priests and philosophers, and large cities where people were free to specialize in industry and other nonagricultural pursuits.

The achievements of the Bantu civilization were thus produced, as it were, part-time. Pottery was made by women when they had the time. Even the "art" of war, which the Bantu, like all civilizations, occasionally practiced, could not be sustained for long periods. If men went to war for more than brief periods, the crops and the herds were neglected, and starvation could result. Only a few men and

237

women were free from the daily task of making a living, and they constituted the government, the small police force or standing army, and the masons, artists, and metallurgists.

In arithmetical terms, the average Bantu farm family could produce enough grain, vegetables, and meat to support themselves plus, at best, a tiny fraction of the amount needed to support a nonfarmer. A family produced perhaps 101 percent to 105 percent of what it needed to live on. In ancient Egypt a farm family, tilling the rich soil along the banks of the Nile, could produce perhaps 150 percent or 200 percent of what it needed, leaving a substantial surplus for the support of philosophers, nobles, priests, stonemasons, brickmakers, artists, and administrators. In modern America a farm family can produce as much as 3,000 percent of what it needs; in other words, twenty to thirty nonfarm families can live on the surplus produced by one farmer.

This means that the economic base of the Bantu civilization was extremely slim. Except in a few regions which had more favorable environments, such as the Interlacustrine area, the more important Bantu states remained small until a trade system had developed. Trade allowed the state to sell its small surplus of gold, copper, iron, ivory, or other products (including slaves at a later period) in exchange for more efficient tools, cloth, luxury goods, and firearms. With these products a king could not only enhance his prestige but could give valued rewards to those subjects and colleagues who served him.

Even where trade brought in this very helpful

wealth, however, the economic base of society severely limited the size of the king's court, his administrative structure, and his army. If he attempted to build up a large standing army of more than a few hundred men, the chances were that there was not enough food to support them, without forcing the commoners to provide more in the form of taxation than they were willing to contribute. One of the factors in Shaka's downfall was the dissatisfaction caused by the expense of maintaining the large, active army on which he built his state.

The result of this economically based fragility was that every Bantu state was limited in how widely it could expand, how many people it could assign to nonagricultural activities, and how large and permanent its capital could become. Once it had reached a certain size and complexity of development, its growth slowed naturally and necessarily. If there were no radical change in environment or contact with different peoples, this stage of development could last indefinitely.

Where new opportunities arose the Bantu peoples seized them readily. In the Interlacustrine Region, isolated though it was, they turned to intensive cultivation of the more fertile soil and produced surpluses which were large compared with those of most of Bantu Africa. As a result, the strength of some of the Bantu kingdoms was substantial, and there was continuing evolution and development in every area of life until the twentieth century and the wholly new challenges it brought. Along the Swahili coast the people absorbed the immigrant Arabs and their knowledge

of the Indian Ocean world. The result was the creation of a series of prosperous cities, a bustling commerce with the outside world, the adoption of Arabic writing, and the building of a graceful civilization which blended Islamic and African ideas. Most of Bantu Africa, however, possessed neither the fertile environment of the Interlacustrine Region nor the continuing contact with the outside world enjoyed by the Swahili coast.

A great question of history is how quickly and effectively the Bantu civilization might have used the influx of ideas, techniques, and materials from Europe to develop its potentialities to higher levels. This question is unlikely ever to be answered, unfortunately, because of the swiftness and totality of the European conquest.

The first contacts between Bantu Africa and Europe seemed useful to Africans, and they might have led, had they taken a different path, to the gradual absorption of Western science and technology within an African cultural framework. Kings of coastal states, who had the first opportunity to trade with Europe, gained a new and important source of income; this enabled them to strengthen their power and add to the effectiveness of their governments. Even far into the interior, in states which had no direct contact with Europeans, participation in the new commercial system stimulated political development. The period of greatest growth in Mwata Yamvo, Mwata Kazembe, Lunda, Bemba, and other interior states followed their involvement in this trading pattern.

The European contact failed to promote growth and development over a longer period, however.

240

As time wore on, its effects proved to be more harmful than helpful.

One injurious effect was the decline of African crafts in the face of competition from cheaper European manufactured goods. African spinning and weaving suffered so severely from the influx of cheaper cloth from Europe and India that they became extinct in many Bantu societies. African iron technology suffered as well. In earlier times an African ironworker might have exchanged a good hoe blade for several pots, baskets of grain, or animals. European hoes were imported at much less expense, however: One ivory tusk or a leopard skin might buy several hoes of good quality. By the end of the nineteenth century many traditional crafts which had been hallmarks of the Bantu civilization had ceased to exist, and Africans were totally dependent upon Europe for many essential articles.

Another serious effect of the European contact was the heightened tensions and rivalries within African states, caused by struggles among various factions to control the trade. Kings whose power had traditionally been secure found their vassals conspiring with each other or with European agents to establish new trade arrangements which would evade the king's regulations and his taxes. Ambitious vassals or clan leaders were emboldened by avarice to attempt coups or revolutions in order to seize the throne. Even though many Bantu kings were able to contain these internal problems, they added to the kings' burdens and problems of statesmanship.

Similarly the European trade intensified rivalries between kingdoms and led to more frequent wars. Since each African state was eager to have the most direct possible access to the European trade, some were willing to resort to war to improve or protect their trading position.

The longer the contact between Africa and Europe, and the more profitable the trade, the more willing Europeans became to intervene in African affairs directly. The sordid history of Portuguese intrigue and intervention in the affairs of Kongo, Ndongo, and Mwene Mutapa, and the seizure and destruction of many Swahili cities, show the lengths to which they were willing to go to insure profits.

In those areas of Bantu Africa where European colonists settled, the negative effects of the European contact were even more vivid. In South Africa the Dutch, and later the British, seized African lands as they expanded. They were, in the process, guilty of trickery, bribery, and outright theft, and they often killed Africans who protested or resisted. White settlement of South Africa was marked by almost constant warfare between the encroaching Europeans and the Africans whose lands they occupied.

Despite these destructive consequences of the European contact, however, much of Bantu Africa

242

was little affected until the nineteenth century. Between about 1480 and 1880 European contact with Bantu Africa was limited to the coastlands, except for shallow penetrations into Kongo, Angola, and Mwene Mutapa and gradual expansion into the interior of South Africa. The mass of Bantu-speaking people in the vast hinterland of Africa knew little of Europe and were touched only indirectly by the African-European trading system. In about 1880, however, this situation changed with lightning speed; between that time and 1900 Europe subjected all of Bantu Africa to colonial rule. This colonial conquest, and the subsequent period of European rule, brought the Bantu civilization under alien control and influence, which has only begun to disappear in the past few years as the new nations achieve independence.

In 1880 European nations, as a result of the rapid industrialization they experienced during the nineteenth century, were engaged in a fierce rivalry for access to raw materials and markets. The factories of England, France, Germany, and other European states needed large supplies of cheap raw materials and customers for their rapidly growing production of a wide variety of manufactured goods. Africa, except for its coastal areas, was the one large area of the world that remained outside the European economic embrace.

European exploration of Africa's interior had begun some years earlier: as early as 1800 in West Africa, and 1850 in Bantu Africa. Between 1860 and 1880 a steady stream of explorers, including David Livingstone, John Speke, Richard Burton, and Henry Morton Stanley, traveled deep into the heart of Bantu Africa, mapping its waterways and landforms and bringing back reports about the people and the goods they produced. From the interior of Rhodesia and Zambia they returned with evidence of mineral wealth. From the upper reaches of the great Congo River they reported large populations, mineral wealth, and vast lands suitable for producing valuable exports such as rubber and palm oil. From the Interlacustrine Region they brought news of great and prosperous kingdoms and a dense population living on fertile lands.

European traders and missionaries began to move into the African interior. European trading posts in the coastal areas began to grow in size, and their agents worked energetically to build a more extensive commerce with the peoples in the interior. Although Portugal dominated the coastal trading stations in most of Angola and Mozambique, and Britain was in clear charge in South Africa, other areas were open to agents from any European company which was interested in joining the competition.

This quickening exploration and commercial expansion was transformed into a scramble by European nations for legal control of African territory when King Leopold II of Belgium proclaimed himself ruler of a vast Congo Free State in 1883. Leopold was acting in a private capacity, as a businessman who headed an international financial combine, and he used the development of a central African commercial empire as a means of increasing his personal wealth and prestige. As king of Belgium, he was subject to political and financial

244

restraints by a democratic parliament; as head of a private corporation which claimed rights to the Congo, he could act with little constraint. This he did boldly and ruthlessly. He secured recognition of his claims from a number of countries (of which the United States was the first) and asserted that his Congo territory included all lands drained by the Congo River system. This proved to cover more than 900,000 square miles, or roughly one-third as much land as that of the United States!

Germany, rivaling Britain as Europe's most important industrial power, had no colonial possessions at the time. But it saw in Africa a chance to become a colonial power, which would give it international prestige as well as control of raw materials and markets. In swift succession it annexed East Africa (Tanganyika), Kamerun (now Cameroun), South-West Africa (now Namibia), and Togoland. Suddenly the scramble began. France quickly moved troops into western Africa, eventually winning international recognition as the ruler of much of northern and western Africa. Britain expanded its South African foothold into what are now Zambia and Rhodesia, and the territories that are now known as Botswana, Lesotho, and Swaziland. In East Africa it seized Egypt and the Sudan, then Kenya, Uganda, and Zanzibar.

In South Africa Britain stepped up its pressures on the Boer republics of the Transvaal and Orange Free State. In 1898 the so-called Boer War broke out, and when it ended with British victory over the settlers of Dutch descent, in 1901, Britain was in legal control of the entire territory that later became the Union of South Africa.

These European seizures of Bantu Africa, between 1883 and 1900, were not accepted passively by Africans. Many African states resisted, and there was a tragic series of bloody wars in Tanganyika, parts of the Congo, Cameroun, South Africa, Rhodesia, and Zambia. After European colonial rule was imposed there were numerous major rebellions. The German-Herero wars in Namibia claimed some 75,000 African lives, nearly half the Herero population. The Maji-Maji rebellion in Tanganyika, in 1904–6, claimed more than 100,000 lives. In Rhodesia the Matabele and Shona, previously hostile to each other, united in a massive uprising against British rule, and lost several thousand lives before they were defeated.

The most horrible suffering in Bantu Africa, however, resulted from the "development" of the Congo Free State by large forces of mercenaries, employed by private companies and the Free State government. Many Africans were forced at gunpoint to abandon their own farms in order to work on great plantations and in mines; those who remained on their own lands were required to produce specified quantities of rubber, cocoa, maize, palm oil, and other cash crops. Those who resisted —and many did—were imprisoned, fined, tortured, maimed, or executed. Within ten years after the establishment of Leopold's government, horrifying reports, usually by missionaries, began to trickle out to the European and American public. But it was not until 1908 that the Belgian Parliament, influenced by protests from many parts of the world, removed the Congo from Leopold's control. At that time the Congo became a Belgian colony, administered by a government responsible to the Belgian Parliament.

Official Belgian investigations of Congo atrocities found that Leopold's agents had been guilty of unbelievably ruthless and inhumane acts. Although it was impossible to assess accurately the number of Congolese who had died through these acts and the starvation that resulted from men being forced to abandon their farms, some authorities believe the figure may have been as high as 3 million. Large areas of the Congo were virtually depopulated by this barbaric campaign, which lasted from 1883 to 1908.

European colonial methods differed from territory to territory. In every territory African resistance to European rule or economic policies was dealt with sternly, although rarely with the brutality used in the Congo. Some features, however, were common to all colonial administrations.

First, Africans were required to acknowledge the sovereignty and ultimate authority of the European colonial government. Some colonial governments followed the policy known as "indirect rule," which used African traditional chiefs and village headmen to carry out government regulations. This was particularly true in the British colonies, although the Portuguese and Germans used indirect rule to a limited extent. In their colonies, however, the more usual pattern was to use European district administrators, backed by armed forces, to rule directly over the people. Under this kind of direct rule African chiefs and kings lost most of their power, and became figureheads whose main function was ceremonial.

247

Second, economic development was given high priority, since the main motivation in the colonial conquest was to gain access to raw materials and to open up consumer markets. Where minerals were found, companies were formed to exploit them. Important cash crops needed in Europe, such as rubber and cotton, were put into production, and African farmers were encouraged (or sometimes forced) to grow them. When force was not used directly, Africans were persuaded to grow cash crops mainly by taxation. Usually a set amount had to be paid, in cash, by each male over sixteen. In order to obtain the money to pay his taxes, a man had either to grow crops for sale or to leave his farm and seek work in the mines or in the towns where Europeans were settling.

Third, the little that was done to aid Africans was done by missionaries, until recent years. Missionaries were encouraged by the colonial governments to provide schools, health care, and religious instruction. The reliance upon missionaries was so widespread that even today many of the independent African governments continue to welcome missionaries and to rely on them to supplement state education, medical services, and community-development activities.

Fourth, the colonial governments paid little respect to African cultures and traditional values. Missionaries were encouraged to convert Africans to Christianity. African religion was dismissed so disparagingly as primitive paganism or animism that the outside world is only now learning that it is based on a Supreme Being and requires its believers to adhere to high moral and ethical stan-

248

dards. African marriage practices, such as polygamy, which were deeply ingrained in the society, were often made illegal if they differed from those of Europeans.

African traditional authorities, the chiefs and kings, lost much of their power in the colonial period. Even where there was indirect rule, the colonial administrators made the important decisions, and removed from office any African officials who were regarded as disloyal or obstructive. Gradually the ordinary African placed less and less faith in his traditional rulers and accepted the colonial government as the source of power. Colonialism so eroded the position of African traditional rulers that today they play almost no role in African government; with the coming of independence in the 1960's a new breed of African leaders, who were educated in European schools or who acquired power in institutions such as labor unions, were the only ones who commanded enough popular respect to govern.

The dominance of Europeans was so complete during the colonial period that it was difficult, even for many Africans, to perceive the good qualities of the Bantu civilization. Many outsiders, and a few Africans, came to believe that the Bantu culture would die, to be replaced by a basically European one. African culture was for so long portrayed as weak and bad, and European culture as strong and good, that it seemed true to many people.

It is now recognized that this view greatly overvalues the quality of Western culture and underestimates the strength and enduring values of Afri-

249

can. The Bantu civilization, which took more than two thousand years to develop, is still very much alive. It is a force which shapes the lives of millions of Africans. It has been changed by colonial rule, and many of its institutions, such as the chieftainship, have been fatally weakened. But its underlying values have not been lost. They shape African views about God, family ties, authority and government, the nature of life, and artistic expression.

No one, not even the most eminent African scholars and philosophers, can predict what the new Bantu civilization of the future will be like. Many decades of enforced Westernization under colonial rule introduced new ideas and destroyed some of the old. Under colonialism the Bantu cultures were, in a sense, anesthetized and partially hidden under the veneer of Western cultural influence and government. With the gaining of independence by Africans, however, and the removal of Western constraints, the vital force of the Bantu civilization is beginning to assert itself. Using Western science and knowledge, it is now rising again, to help Bantu-speaking Africans create a future for themselves which will be a blend of old and new, indigenous and imported.

Today the majority of the Bantu peoples live in independent nations, ruled by their own leaders, free to begin the long task of reconstructing and modernizing the Bantu civilization. But in five states —Angola, Mozambique, Namibia, Rhodesia, and South Africa—they are still firmly under the control of Europeans, and their destiny is in the hands of these alien minorities who control the govern-

250

ments, the wealth, and the military power. Yet even in these five states the Bantu-speaking Africans are restless, and seek opportunities to remove the yokes which restrain them. They have organized aggressive freedom movements in Angola, Mozambique, and Rhodesia, and are prevented from doing so in Namibia and South Africa only by the enormous power of European police systems.

The modern history of the African struggle against colonial rule, which resulted in independence for most Africans, suggests that the Africans of these alien-ruled countries will continue to seek the self-determination that their kinsmen on the rest of the continent have achieved. If so, then they will someday join other members of the Bantu civilization in building a new way of life that is modern, yet blends in the proud heritage of their ancient past.

Statue at library of National University of Zaire

*Modern Bakuba cup,
by D. Bakala,
Kinshasa, 1960*

Bibliography

While there is a rich literature on the Bantu-speaking peoples and on modern southern Africa, much of it is either very technical or concerned with controversial political disputes. The brief reading list below has been carefully selected to provide the reader with information that is more detailed than that in this book, and that covers a wide area of interest. Although most of the recommended books are written for younger readers, several are quite challenging. Many of the recommended books themselves contain extensive bibliographies that will help the interested reader to go even further into detail in archeology, history, cultures, and political affairs.

AXELSON, E. (translator and editor), *South-East Africa, 1488–1530.* Toronto: Longmans, Green and Company, 1940. Useful translations of chronicles of early Portuguese explorers and mariners, now out of print and hard to find.

BALANDIER, GEORGES, *Daily Life in the Kingdom of the Kongo*. New York: Pantheon Books, 1968. Although slightly difficult to read, a valuable account of Kongo history and culture.

BUTCHER, T. K., *The Great Explorations, Africa*. London: Denis Dobson, 1959. Accounts of a number of explorations, written for younger readers.

COLE, ERNEST, *House of Bondage*. New York: Random House, 1967. A beautiful and informative collection of photographs, by a Black South African, of the oppressed African people.

CRANE, LOUISE, *The Land and People of the Congo*. New York: J. B. Lippincott Company, 1971. Written for young adult readers, a good general account of modern Zaire and its peoples.

CUNNISON, I. G., *The Luapula Peoples of Northern Rhodesia*. Manchester, England: Manchester University Press, 1959. An anthropological work on the history and culture of the eastern Lunda.

DAVIDSON, BASIL, *The African Past*. Boston: Little, Brown and Company, 1964. A useful anthology which includes many original documents by both Europeans and Africans on various aspects of African history.

————, *Black Mother*. Boston: Little, Brown and Company, 1964. A very good description of the origins and conduct of the infamous slave trade.

————, *Discovering Our African Heritage*. Boston: Ginn and Company, 1971. Although produced as a textbook, this is a very readable and useful general account of African history for young adults, with good sections on southern Africa and the Bantu-speaking peoples.

————, *East and Central Africa to the Late Nineteenth Century*. London: Longmans, Green and Company, 1967. Written with the assistance of J. E. F. Mhina, an African historian, and the advice of B. A. Ogot, a very distinguished African history professor, this quite readable and useful book was produced as a textbook for African high school students. It covers most of the Bantu-speaking peoples.

DIETZ, BETTY, and OLATUNJI, MICHAEL, *Musical Instruments of Africa*. New York: The John Day Company, 1965. Descriptions and pictures of numerous musical instruments, including those of the Bantu-speaking peoples.

ELTING, MARY, and McKOWN, ROBIN, *A Mongo Homecoming*. New York: M. Evans and Company, 1969. A story of family life and culture of one Bantu-speaking group, written for younger readers.

FAGAN, BRIAN, *Southern Africa*. London: Thames and Hudson, 1965. Although somewhat technical, this well written and illustrated book is the best published account of the archeology and early history of the region south of the Zambezi River. Highly recommended.

FREEMAN-GRENVILLE, G. S. P., *The East African Coast*. Oxford: The Clarendon Press, 1962. A very useful anthology of Arabic, Portuguese, and African documents on the history of the East African coastal area.

GREENLEE, W. B. (translator), *The Voyage of Pedro Alvares Cabral to Brazil and India*. London: Hakluyt Society, 1938. Although hard to find, this is an interesting and informative account of one of the earliest Portuguese mariners on the East African coast.

HALLETT, ROBIN, *The Penetration of Africa*. New York: Frederick A. Praeger Publishers, 1965. The first half of this book is a useful account of how and why Europe sought to explore Africa—useful even though explorations of Bantu Africa are not covered.

HOLLADAY, VIRGINIA, *Bantu Tales*. New York: The Viking Press, 1970. Legends and folktales of the Luba, Lulua, and other Bantu-speaking peoples of Zaire.

KIRKMAN, JAMES S., *Men and Monuments on the East African Coast.* New York: Frederick A. Praeger Publishers, 1966. A valuable archeological work on the coast of East Africa, with many rare photographs of ruins and sites.

MARSH, ZOE, and KINGNORTH, G. W., *An Introduction to the History of East Africa.* Cambridge: Cambridge University Press, 1966. Prepared for high school use in East Africa or England, this is a useful work, though not as good as the similar book by Basil Davidson cited above.

MURDOCK, GEORGE P., *Africa: Its Peoples and Their Culture History.* New York: McGraw-Hill Book Company, 1959. Out of print, technical, and controversial, this book is the most comprehensive "encyclopedia" of anthropological information on all the peoples of Africa ever written; it is an invaluable reference book.

MURPHY, E. JEFFERSON, *History of African Civilization.* New York: Thomas Y. Crowell Company, 1972. Written for general readers, this work provides a broad historical account for all Africa, including Bantu Africa.

——, *Understanding Africa.* New York: Thomas Y. Crowell Company, 1969. A useful general introduction to Africa written for young adult readers.

NOLEN, BARBARA (editor), *Africa is Thunder and Wonder.* New York: Charles Scribner's Sons, 1972. A good anthology of literature by African writers, including several well-known Bantu-speaking authors writing in English.

——, *Africa Is People.* New York: E. P. Dutton and Company, 1967. An anthology on culture, thought, and history by modern writers.

OLIVER, ROLAND and CAROLINE (editors), *Africa in the*

Days of Exploration. Englewood Cliffs, N.J.: Prentice-Hall, 1965. Selections from the journals of explorers.

PATON, ALAN, *The Land and People of South Africa*. New York: J. B. Lippincott Company, 1972 (revised edition). A general book on modern South Africa, written by the prominent liberal South African novelist.

RAVENSTEIN, E. G. (translator), *Journal of the First Voyage of Vasco da Gama, 1497–1499*. London: Hakluyt Society, 1938. Available only in large libraries, an interesting account of da Gama's voyage and impressions of coastal Africa.

SCHAPERA, I., *The Bantu-Speaking Tribes of South Africa*. Cape Town: Maskew Miller, 1950. Rather technical, but a useful work on the cultures of the southern Bantu-speaking peoples by a prominent anthropologist.

SHINNIE, PETER (editor), *The African Iron Age*. Oxford: The Clarendon Press, 1971. Summaries by leading archeologists of the findings of their science as of about 1970; useful sections on the Bantu-speaking peoples.

SIMMONS, JACK, *Livingstone and Africa*. New York: Collier Books, 1962. A useful introduction to the life and career of David Livingstone, with a bibliography of his journals, and commentary on various Bantu-speaking peoples whom he visited.

STANLEY, E. J. (editor), *The Three Voyages of Vasco da Gama*. London: Hakluyt Society, date unknown. Hard to find, but contains helpful information on all of da Gama's explorations.

STERLING, THOMAS, *Exploration of Africa*. New York: American Heritage Publishing Company, 1963. A fairly useful account and anthology, for young-adult and general readers.

THEAL, G. M., *Records of South-Eastern Africa* (9 vol-

257

umes). London: Frank Cass, 1969. Originally published in 1898 and reprinted in 1969, these volumes,
obtainable only in large libraries, provide a massive
collection of accounts by mariners and explorers.

TURNBULL, COLIN, *The Peoples of Africa*. Cleveland:
World Publishing Company, 1962. Written by a
popular anthropologist, this general work contains
moderately useful information on African peoples,
including those of the Bantu-speaking family.

VANSINA, JAN, *Kingdoms of the Savanna*. Madison: University of Wisconsin Press, 1968. Difficult to read in
places, this is still an excellent account of the history and life of many of the more important Bantu-
speaking states, including Luba and Lunda.

VLAHOS, OLIVIA, *African Beginnings*. New York: The
Viking Press, 1967. A general work on African history and prehistory, with several chapters on the
Bantu-speaking peoples, written for young-adult
and general readers.

Index

(Page numbers in italics indicate illustrations.)

About the Author

E. Jefferson Murphy was for many years Executive Vice President of the African-American Institute, a major United States private organization established to promote African development and African-American understanding. As a representative of AAI, he lived in Africa for nearly seven years, and has made frequent trips to all parts of the African continent, as well as to Europe and the Pacific Islands.

Born in Georgia, Mr. Murphy received his B.A. and M.A. degrees from Emory University in Atlanta and his Ph.D. from the University of Connecticut. He has taught sociology and anthropology at Emory University, the University of North Carolina, and the University College of Fort Hare, Union of South Africa, and is at present a member of the Columbia University Faculty Seminar on Africa. Mr. Murphy serves as a consultant to various philanthropic foundations, colleges, and secondary schools, and as a trustee of the Museum of African Art in Washington, D.C. He is the author of *Understanding Africa* and *History of African Civilization,* and is now at work on a number of other projects, including a survey of Carnegie Corporation programs in Africa, Asia, and the Caribbean, and a book on the education of Africans in the Republic of South Africa. With his wife and three children he lives in Cos Cob, Connecticut, where he enjoys fishing, boating, and skiing.

About the Illustrator

Louise Jefferson's knowledge of African art and culture is the result of extensive travel in Africa, twice on Ford Foundation Fellowships and once as a representative of the African-American Institute at a southern African art conference.

A well-known cartographer and calligrapher, Miss Jefferson served for many years as art director with Friendship Press, the publishing division of the Missionary Education Movement. She has been a map consultant for the New York State Council for the Arts and a consultant and art coordinator for the New York City Board of Education's special African Project. She has written and illustrated a reference book on the decorative arts of Africa.

Miss Jefferson studied at Howard University, Hunter College, and Columbia University. She now lives in Litchfield, Connecticut.